Does Israel Have a Future?

Does Israel Have a Future?

The Case for a Post-Zionist State

Constance Hilliard

Foreword by Norton Mezvinsky

Potomac Books, Inc.
Washington, D.C.

Library of Congress Cataloging-in-Publication Data
Hilliard, Constance B.
  Does Israel have a future? : the case for a post-Zionist state / Constance Hilliard. —
1st ed.
     p. cm.
  Includes bibliographical references and index.
  ISBN 978-1-59797-234-5 (hardcover : alk. paper)
  1. Arab-Israeli conflict—1993– 2. Israel—Politics and government—20th century.
3. Israel—Politics and government—21st century. 4. Palestinian Arabs—Politics and
government—20th century. 5. Palestinian Arabs—Politics and government—21st
century. 6. Post-Zionism. I. Title.
  DS119.76.H55 2009
  320.54095694—dc22
                                    2009021959

Printed in the United States of America on acid-free paper that meets the American National Standards Institute Z39-48 Standard.

Potomac Books, Inc.
22841 Quicksilver Drive
Dulles, Virginia 20166

First Edition

10 9 8 7 6 5 4 3 2 1

To Howard James Whitaker

"No problem can be solved from the same consciousness that created it. We must learn to see the world anew."

—ALBERT EINSTEIN

Contents

Acknowledgments

I would first like to express gratitude to my agent, Jodie Rhodes, without whose encouragement and professional skill this book would have remained a twenty-page proposal locked away in a desk drawer. I am also grateful to my colleagues in the history department at the University of North Texas (UNT), who offered thoughtful advice, kindly given, even when their views differed from mine. Historian William Wilson, recently retired from the department, possesses a greater breadth of intellectual knowledge than anyone I know. His help in keeping this book on track was invaluable.

Senior editor at Potomac Books, Hilary Claggett, and her hard working staff have been wonderful with whom to work. This book has also given me the opportunity to get to know Dr. Norton Mezvinsky, whose faith in the project carried it through its most difficult moments. I am also indebted to the gentle urging of Emily Wachsmann, a graduate student at UNT and promising young scholar, who believed in the book long before anyone else did.

The thanking of spouses and significant others in the "Acknowledgements" had always seemed to me a rote requirement of authors wishing to maintain domestic tranquility. That is, until now. My husband, Terrill Tripp, saved this project and he did so more than once. At times, anxiety about writing a book on so controversial a subject as Israel's future nearly paralyzed me. Whenever that happened, I would announce to my husband that I was abandoning the project and he would sit me down and give me "the talk." Terrill reminded me that the book's message came from my heart. He would say that I simply had to honor that fact, if I were ever to have the least modicum of inner peace (and he were to have a household free from the frustrations of an intellectually/soul-constipated wife.). I now understand that there is no power on earth stronger and more inspiring than a loving and supportive family. I am, indeed, grateful for the support of my husband and the patience of my son.

Foreword

When Israeli prime minister Benjamin Netanyahu met with President Barack Obama in the spring of 2009, the Israeli leader did not mention "Palestinian state" even once. However, he did utter the term after returning home. But what Netanyahu described was a decapitated state in which Israel would actually retain sovereignty, have the right to interfere at any time it disagreed with Palestinian policies, and use military force when necessary to accomplish those ends. This has actually been the position of the Israeli government since the end of the 1970s when Menachem Begin used the wording "autonomous rule" for Palestinians, as the Israeli government had not yet entered the term "Palestinian state" into its political lexicon. Not surprisingly, those Palestinians who have advocated the establishment of such a state in the past find the Israeli conception of a non-sovereign political entity, dependent on Israel for its viability, ludicrous.

Even more telling of Israel's refusal to be bound by U.S. diplomatic ethics was the fact that the Israeli prime minister, shortly after returning home from the meeting with President Obama, announced the expansion of an Israeli settlement in the Palestinian territories, which he couched in terms of "natural growth." The Israeli prime minister's actions were in direct opposition to President Obama's declaration, seconded by Secretary of State Hillary Clinton, that all plans for expanding Jewish settlements in the Arab Occupied Territories be frozen.

The Obama administration's admonitions may have been spoken too softly and without the forcefulness needed to make Netanyahu take heed. More than 400,000 Jewish settlers have already appropriated lands in the Palestinian West Bank for Jewish-only settlements. In addition, Israel continues to control border crossings, roads, and water rights in the Palestinian areas. The notion of a two-state solution in which Israel agrees to live side by side with an independent Palestinian nation is not only a fiction, but an increasingly dangerous one.

Professor Hilliard has laid out a narrative that helps us to recognize why the United States can no longer afford to delude itself into believing that a two-state solution is a viable option for Middle East peace. Israel is a work in progress. It will never be a safe haven for the Jewish people until it reaches a level of maturity allowing it to embrace the creation of a single binational state of all Israel's people, Jewish as well as Arab, with no one group being privileged over the others.

From the beginnings of political Zionism in the late nineteenth century, Jewish settlement in the Holy Land was met with Arab riots. Israel's enemies during the early decades after its founding consisted of the Palestinians displaced by the Jewish state and the surrounding Arab states. But even as Israel has created one of the largest and most efficient armies in the world, its military victories have led to what can only be described as a disastrous nexus of unintended consequences. Humiliation of the Arabs after the 1967 Six-Day War fueled a Muslim backlash and the emergence of a far more lethal danger to Israel—extreme, radical Islam. Where once the Jewish state contended with Arab enemies numbering in the hundreds of millions, it now must tackle the enmity of a large portion of the world's 1.5 billion Muslims. This book also reminds us that the West did the Jews no favor by supporting Zionist aspirations for a Jewish homeland in Palestine after World War II, rather than opening up their own borders to Jewish emigration.

As Hilliard points out, the two-state solution will not accomplish the ultimate goal—security for Israeli Jews and justice for the Palestinians. She also offers compelling evidence that time is not on the side of the Jewish state, and "denial of the inevitable" on the part of a community once victimized by the Holocaust is a dangerous creed. Fundamentalists of all stripes have converged on the region, hoping to hasten apocalyptic upheaval.

Sometime ago, the eminent Jewish intellectual and scientist Albert Einstein argued (as did the great Jewish philosopher Martin Buber and others) that a binational state of joint sovereignty with "complete equality of rights between the two partners" should be established. Such a state in historic Palestine, declared Einstein, would be predicated on "the love of their homeland that the two people share." Indeed, many Jews like myself have been and are now opposed in varying ways to Zionism and its principles. Among both religiously oriented and secular Jews, there exist differing interpretations of what the term "Jewish state" means and/or should mean. I—and other Jews like me—reject categorically the concept of an exclusivist, Jewish, Zionist state and therefore oppose the Zionist character and oppressive actions of the state of Israel.

The time has come for the international community, led by the United States, to embrace this powerful concept of a democratic secular state replacing the exclusivist Jewish state of Israel. Such changes will not happen overnight. But they will finally put Israel on the path of peace rather than that of perpetual warfare. In such a state, Jews and non-Jews would have equal rights and privileges. Both Arab and Jewish histories and identities would be respected and protected. Israel-Palestine would be without walls, fences, and checkpoints, without Jews-only roads and Jews-only settlements. There would still be a thriving Hebrew culture but also a Levantine Arab culture. Surely, we as Americans will see our interests better served by using our position as the world's sole superpower to uphold a future Israeli constitution that protects the rights and interests of all.

Dr. Norton Mezvinsky
Distinguished University Professor Emeritus of History
Central Connecticut State University & President & CEO
International Council for Middle East Studies, Inc.
Washington, D.C.

Preface

When the world learned about the Holocaust, there was an outpouring of emotional support for Jews, but not a single country opened its borders to take in the survivors. America had enough land to support millions. But given the fact that it had just emerged from the Great Depression, it did not have enough heart to do so. Five decades later, when suicide bombers launched the September 11, 2001, attacks on the United States, bewildered Americans asked why Arabs hate us. It all started back then.

This book will show how a trap was set for Israel at the time of its founding. It was not built of barbed wire and scrap metal, but rather from the demographics of the region and shards of the West's own anti-Semitism. This trap has myriad trip wires and phantom doors, but only one escape. And time is running out.

The question today is where will Israel be two, five, ten years from now? Will there even be a Jewish state, given the forces ranged against it? This is one of the most explosive issues of our times, and *the American foreign policy establishment refuses to talk about it.*

Jewish and Arab Israelis discuss their future a lot. The issue of whether Zionism should be replaced by a post-Zionist state that welcomes all people, rather than one that privileges only the Jews, has gripped the airwaves, newspapers, and café conversations. These discussions are some of the most meaningful to engage the Jewish state since its inception. Jewish Studies Programs in American universities also discuss these vital issues in sometimes painstaking detail. However, America's political establishment has until now backed away from engaging this subject in any meaningful way. And yet what happens to the Jewish people, in the wake of the Holocaust, and the Palestinian people displaced by Israel will constitute the greatest moral issue of our time. Israel is also the geopolitical linchpin of our Middle East policy, and what happens to that tiny, vulnerable nation will have a pivotal impact on America's place on the world stage. Of even greater urgency is the fact that Israel possesses nuclear weapons and Iran may be building them. If feeling cornered, the Jewish state may well decide to use them against its oil-producing Muslim neighbors. So shouldn't we be talking about, debating, trying to understand the dynamics that drive Israel's history, and preparing for all eventualities as we might any other potentially earth-shattering event?

I have written *Does Israel Have a Future?* in the hope that some will recognize as I do that while the Palestinians have suffered the most casualties in this conflict, it is the Jewish people who are now in greater danger than they've ever been in before. Most talking heads who flood the airwaves with their strategic-sounding analyses are doing little more than soothing the anxiety of Israel's supporters with magical thinking. In contrast, my book offers a clear lens for seeing the urgency of Israel's plight. It will reveal:

- How the United States and its allies, having been unable to protect Jews from the Holocaust, appeared to accede to Zionist demands for a Jewish state in 1948, but in fact embedded a time bomb within the heart of the new nation of Israel.
- How that time bomb threatens Israel in ways that are not being addressed
- Why America's Middle East peace initiatives are exercises in futility
- Why the crisis in the Middle East may be pushing the Jewish people toward a new Holocaust, about which most people are in deep denial
- Why there is still some hope for the future if actions are taken now

- What kind of actions are needed to make Israel a place of spiritual renewal and peace, rather than a permanent military fortress.

In recent years I have seen some of the most vibrant, provocative, and insightful scholarship in the academic world published on the subject of Israel and the Middle East conflict. As a consequence, I waited for someone else—an Israeli perhaps, an American Jew, a Palestinian, or at the very least, someone more extroverted and less private than I to write *this* book, an honest, straightforward assessment of what *really* lies ahead for the Jewish state. In 1979 I became foreign policy adviser to Sen. John Tower of Texas, who also chaired the Senate Armed Services Committee. After traveling in the Middle East and immersing myself in intelligence reports, I began to suspect that Israel's situation might be far more precarious than the U.S. foreign policy establishment was willing to admit. But in the early 1980s my first husband was tortured to death in the Angolan civil war. Suddenly, and for the next two decades, my attention was riveted on African rather than on Middle Eastern political developments. My concerns for Israel are rooted in the fact that I have experienced at close range political disintegration in a way most Americans only read about in the news media

And then, I found myself one November afternoon in 2007, in Washington, D.C., with three hours to spare between meetings. That semester, I had begun teaching a new course at the University of North Texas called "The History of Violence." Even though history is usually studied on the scale of a human lifetime or even that of centuries, this course allowed me to explore with my students whatever insights recorded history reveal in regard to whether ethnic cleansing and genocide might be preventable social phenomena. That afternoon, I took a taxi to the National Mall and got out at the Fourteenth Street entrance to the United States Holocaust Memorial Museum. I can't say what I expected to see or feel or learn upon entering the building. But the exhibits transported me not just to the nightmare of World War II Europe, but also to an inner landscape of my being that I had never before explored. For what seemed like hours, I stood paralyzed before a mound of 4,000 shoes left behind by victims at the Majdanek camp in Poland. How could shoes, emptied of their human inhabitants and therefore nearly weightless, grind heel marks into my soul? But they did. I eventually moved on to other exhibits. I sat for what seemed like a fleeting infinity in the Hall of Remembrance, a hexagonal-shaped room, meditating on a mantra that kept intruding upon my thoughts. How could the world have ignored the signs and not seen the Holocaust or Shoah, which is the Hebrew word for this monstrous calamity, coming? At the close of the tour, I stepped back into the late afternoon chill, no closer to answering that question. But one thing I did know. I would write this book, no matter what.

It may seem presumptuous to suggest what Israelis should do with their country. But I refuse to back away from the most pressing moral imperative of our times, however fearful I may be that some who read this book will misinterpret my words and my motives. Israel's future is not just about Palestinians, Jews, Israelis, Arabs and Muslims. It is about whether concerned Americans wish to have the horrors of a new Holocaust etched across our collective souls, when the signs of impending disaster are as clear as a mile-high billboard. And thus, I apologize in advance if I may have trampled on the unspoken etiquette surrounding the discourse on Israel for I have refused to embed my message in complex prose and intellectualizations. If this book reads with a naked urgency, it is because I fear that time is of the essence.

I have neither family nor religious ties that bind me to the Middle East. I am a practicing Buddhist. Much of what I know about Semitic languages and history I learned from a German Jew and Harvard lecturer who narrowly escaped the Holocaust. During my college years, Professor Ilse Lichtenstadter became more than a professor to me. This remarkable woman became a loving grandmother. In the presence of her goading intellect, emotional generosity, and quiet woundedness, new insights seeped into my consciousness. One was the answer to a question that had often perplexed me as an American of African descent: who but your own people really cares if you live or die? What I learned from my relationship with Ilse Lichtenstadter and now grasp at the deepest level of my being is that our true friends are not always the ones who tell us what we want to hear. This book is written in recognition of that fact.

1

Lock out

On May 13, 1939, a roster of 937 refugees fleeing Nazi persecution set sail for Cuba aboard the SS *St. Louis*, an ocean liner on the Hamburg-America Line. The majority of these refugees were German and 936 were Jewish. The government of Cuba, under President Frederico Laredo Brú, refused to allow the ship to dock. The pro-Nazi editor of *Diario de la Marina,* Havana's oldest newspaper, falsely claimed that the ship's Jewish passengers were communist subversives.[1] As the vessel turned away and sailed up the North American coast, the U.S. Coast Guard patrolled the waters to ensure that none of the desperate refugees jumped ship. While President Franklin D. Roosevelt had expressed sympathy for the ship's Jewish passengers, Secretary of State Cordell Hull and Southern Democrats vehemently opposed allowing them entry into the United States. Some even threatened to oppose Roosevelt's 1940 re-election bid.

Forced to return to Europe, many of the passengers perished in the Holocaust. This incident became immortalized in the 1976 film *Voyage of the Damned*, directed by Stuart Rosenberg and nominated for three Academy Awards.

Évian Conference

The year before the failed voyage, President Roosevelt had arranged the Évian Conference—a meeting of thirty-two Western nations in Évian-les-Bains, France. The only item on the agenda was what to do about Jews fleeing persecution in Nazi Germany and Eastern Europe. However, the conference participants, while expressing sympathy for the refugees, were unable to agree on a resolution condemning the Germans' treatment of Jews. The Roosevelt administration, fearing a public backlash in difficult economic times, refused to allow any more Jews into the United States than those covered under German and Austrian immigration quotas. The British delegate, led by Sir Edward Turnour, a prominent member of Parliament, insisted that Britain was overpopulated but that the nation might find space for a small number of refugees in its British territories in East Africa. The Australian delegate, Thomas Walter White, noted, ". . . having no real racial problem, we are not desirous of importing one by encouraging any scheme of large-scale foreign migration." The French delegate, Victor Henry Bérenger, stated that France had reached "the extreme point of saturation as regards admission of refugees."

The Évian Conference did establish the Intergovernmental Committee on Refugees (ICR), which had the task of trying to persuade individual countries to take in Jewish refugees as permanent residents. However, committee members lacked the necessary special authority and were therefore unable to make headway in settling the growing number of displaced persons.

Professor Theodore S. Hamerow, in *Why We Watched: Europe, America, and the Holocaust*, described the complex workings of anti-Semitism within the United States and other Western countries. It was their own unresolved prejudices in regard to the Jews that slowed the response of these nations to fleeing refugees. In fact, the only nation volunteering at the Évian Conference to take in Jews was the Dominican Republic, whose dictator, Rafael Leonidas Trujillo Molina, offered to grant tracts of land to 100,000 Jewish farmers.[2] Throughout the war period, Professor Hamerow noted:

> . . . the states of Latin America accepted more Jewish refugees than
> many of the nations with a more advanced economy and a stronger
> commitment to the principles of democracy, for even in those countries

that condemned the doctrines of National Socialism most loudly there were the familiar anti-Semitic prejudices and resentments.[3]

The Brazilian case was more complex. Jeffrey Lesser, a professor at Emory University and author of *Welcoming the Undesirables: Brazil and the Jewish Question*, discovered that after having opened its borders to Jewish immigration at the turn of the twentieth century, the Brazilian government placed a secret ban on Jews fleeing Nazi persecution in 1937. The ban was lifted a year later, and more Jews relocated to that nation than ever before. According to Professor Lesser, the Brazilian elites held contradictory images of Jews. Jewish leaders may have manipulated those stereotypes to their advantage.[4]

Attitudes toward Jews
The Germans took special note of the fact that none of the countries condemning them for anti-Semitism accepted Jews into their countries. Adolf Hitler remarked in a speech at the Reichstag:

> It is a shameful spectacle to see how the whole democratic world is oozing sympathy for the poor tormented Jewish people, but remains hard hearted and obdurate when it comes to helping them which is surely, in view of its attitude, an obvious duty.[5]

In fact, a 1938 opinion poll revealed that 68 percent of Americans opposed admitting large numbers of refugees from Germany and Austria into the United States. In January 1939, 83 percent of the American public opposed a bill that would allow European Jewish refugees to enter the country. "Jews were not like most Americans, real Americans" was the view taken by the U.S. public, according to Professor Hamerow. He added:

> Surveys of public opinion show, moreover, that distrust of Jews actually increased during the war years. Asked which national, religious, or social groups in the United States were a threat to the country—Jews, Negroes, Catholics, Germans, or Japanese—a plurality of respondents consistently named the Jews, more even than the Germans.[6]

Even the possibility of admitting Jewish refugee children above the regular quota limits died in congressional committee. That same year, the Veterans of Foreign Wars, even while aware of the plight of European Jews, passed a resolution calling for a halt to immigration for a ten-year period. Francis H. Kinnicutt represented thirty "patriotic" organizations, including the American Legion and Daughters of the American Revolution, all of which campaigned to keep Jewish refugees out of the United States. Kinnicutt declared in his congressional testimony:

> . . . this is just part of a drive to go back to the condition when we were flooded with foreigners who tried to run the country on different lines from those laid down by the old stock. . . . Strictly speaking, it is not a refugee bill at all, for by the nature of the case most of those admitted would be of the Jewish race.[7]

Depression Wounds
It would be easy to look back on this period as one guided solely by cold, unfeeling, Western anti-Semitism toward the Jews. But it should be remembered that the defining event of the 1930s for the United States and much of the global economy was the Great Depression. It was marked by the stock market crash of 1929, which set in motion turmoil in financial markets around the world. This included a run on the banks that subsequently failed, a catastrophic loss of jobs, a steep decline in wages and values, and difficulty securing personal and business credit. By 1933 American unemployment rates hovered in the 25 percent range.

Other nations were hit even more severely. Great Britain suffered a 50 percent devaluation of export earnings, with unemployment in the shipbuilding areas of the nation areas rising to 70 percent. Professor Patricia Clavin at the University of Keele in Great Britain observed:

> In much of central and eastern Europe, as in the Weimar Republic [Germany], when politicians from moderate, centrist parties (Liberals, Conservatives, Democratic Socialists) failed to introduce policies to tackle the crisis, they lost out to extremist parties to the Right and Left of the political spectrum.[8]

Adolf Hitler and his Nazi Party came to power in 1933, having broadened their initial appeal among disgruntled World War I veterans to middle-class Germans who had seen their savings accounts wiped out by inflation and a devaluation of their currency. The country's unemployment rate had risen to 30 percent.

At the beginning of World War II, the U.S. economy was just beginning to recover and still suffered unemployment in the 17 percent range. Not surprisingly, the dismal economic picture militated against admitting Jews or anybody else over and above the immigration quotas.

The "Jewish Problem"
Europeans in the pre–World War II era often made reference to "the "Jewish Problem." " But what exactly was this so-called dilemma? Anti-Semitism compounded tensions created by job competition among diverse ethnic groups. This complex theology of Jewish hatred and scapegoating had existed throughout European history. Jews were accused of being responsible for the death of Jesus Christ and refusing to assimilate into Christian cultural values—maintaining their distinct identity as Jews and being unwilling to convert. However, around the turn of the twentieth century, anti-Semitism evolved into a more secularized, more virulent strain, which maintained that Jewish cabals were secretly trying to take over the world. The famous Russian novelist Fyodor Dostoyevsky wrote in 1877:

> It is not for nothing that . . . the Jews are reigning everywhere over stock-exchanges; it is not for nothing that they control capital, that they are the masters of credit, and it is not for nothing—I repeat—that they are also the masters of international politics, and what is going to happen in the future is known to the Jews themselves: their reign, their complete reign is approaching! We are approaching the complete triumph of ideas before which sentiments of humanity, thirst for truth, Christian and national feelings, and even those of national dignity, must bow. On the contrary, we are approaching materialism, a blind, carnivorous craving for personal material welfare, a craving for personal accumulation of money by any means—this is all that has been proclaimed as the supreme aim, as the reasonable thing, as liberty, in lieu of the Christian idea of salvation only through the closest moral and brotherly fellowship of men.[9]

Emigration and Expulsion

In the period leading up to World War II, the Nazis' first plan for dealing with the Jewish Problem was to pressure them to leave Germany. Initially, Jews were allowed to bring their possessions with them, even though a heavy emigration tax and restrictions on the amount of money they could take out of the country were later imposed in the fall of 1941. The Nazi official in charge of Jewish affairs, Karl Adolf Eichmann, made a tour of European capitals in 1937, searching for a venue to which the Jews could be deported. However, Britain, Canada, Belgium, the Netherlands, and Switzerland refused to accept these Jews, even though most were middle class and some were wealthy. The European nations argued that high unemployment prevented them from absorbing these refugees. Australia, meanwhile, insisted that an acceptance of non-Aryan immigrants would destabilize its society's racial balance.[10]

Eichmann then traveled to Palestine in September 1937 with his superior, Herbert Hagen, to investigate the possibility of deporting Jews to that part of the world. Unable to obtain an entry visa from the British authorities in Haifa, they traveled to Cairo where they met with Feival Polkes, an agent of the Jewish paramilitary organization, Haganah. Polkes tried to persuade them to push for European Jewish immigration to Palestine. But, in the report to the Nazi government after the trip, Eichmann and Hagen rejected Polkes' proposal, citing the cost and their disinclination to support the creation of a Zionist state.

With the annexation of Austria in 1938, Eichmann was sent to Vienna to set up the Central Office for Jewish Emigration. Over the course of the next year, this operation oversaw the expulsion of 110,000 Austrian Jews. According to the account of a Jewish leader named Franz Mayer, Eichmann developed a fast-moving assembly line process:

> You put in a Jew at one end, with property, a shop, a bank account, and legal rights. He passed through the building and came out at the other end without property, without privileges, without rights, with nothing except a passport and order to leave the country within a fortnight; otherwise, he would find himself inside a concentration camp.[11]

Within six months of the annexation, 45,000 Jews had left the country; another 100,000 emigrated before the outbreak of World War II.

Eichmann received high marks in Nazi circles for efficiency. Still, German officials were frustrated by the difficulties they were having in getting other countries to accept these emigrants. The population of European Jews at that time was 11 million. Unwilling even to fill already established quotas, the United States admitted only 100,000, England 80,000, Holland 22,000, Belgium about 13,000, Switzerland 9000, Argentina 20,000, other Latin American countries about 20,000, and British-controlled Palestine 70,000.[12]

By June 1940, the German Foreign Ministry was looking for faster, more decisive ways of ridding the newly acquired territories on their eastern flank of millions of Jewish inhabitants. A new plan was devised, calling for the forced migration of all European Jews to the island of Madagascar, a French colonial possession off the east coast of Africa. Eichmann declared in an August 1940 memorandum that four million Jews be settled on that island. Because the plan was contingent on the Nazis gaining control of the British navy and using captured British naval ships for transport, this plan was never implemented.

The "Final Solution"

It was only after previous plans to rid Germany of the Jews and the tide of the war began to turn against Germany that Hitler instituted the "Final Solution"—the extermination camps.[13] On January 20, 1942, Reinhard Heydrich, the second in command of the Waffen-SS, convened a conference at the Berlin suburb of Wannsee with fifteen top Nazi bureaucrats. The goal of the meeting was to coordinate the Final Solution, or *Die Endlösung*, in which "Europe would be combed of Jews from east to west," according to a statement made by Heydrich at the conference.[14] The initial plan called for the deportation of Jews to Eastern Europe, where they would be used for hard labor in the construction of roads and bridges. Those who did not die from the harsh conditions would then be annihilated in death camps. However, the Nazis were confronted with unexpected difficulties on the Soviet front, which led them to abandon the idea of putting together Jewish work crews in favor of opening death camps immediately.

In October 1943 Heydrich's boss, Heinrich Himmler, gave a speech at a meeting in Posen, Poland, in which he disclosed the true meaning of the Final Solution. Himmler declared:

I also want to refer here very frankly to a very difficult matter. We can now very openly talk about this among ourselves, and yet we will never discuss this publicly . . . I am now referring to the evacuation of the Jews, to the extermination of the Jewish people. This is something that is easily said: "The Jewish people will be exterminated," says every Party member, "this is very obvious, it is in our program—elimination of the Jews, extermination, a small matter." And then they turn up, the up-standing 80 million Germans, and each one has his decent Jew. They say the others are all pigs, but this particular one is a splendid Jew. (compare with Rosenstrasse protest) But none has observed it, endured it. Most of you here know what it means when 100 corpses lie next to each other, when there are 500 or when there are 1,000. To have endured this and at the same time to have remained a decent person— with exceptions due to human weaknesses—has made us tough, and is a glorious chapter that has not and will not be spoken of. Because we know how difficult it would be for us if we will have had Jews as secret saboteurs, agitators and rabble rousers in every city, what with the bomb- ings, with the burden and with the hardships of the war. If the Jews were still part of the German nation, we would most likely arrive now at the state we were at in 1916/17.[15]

The Nazis set up six major extermination camps in Poland—Aushwitz- Birkenau, Chelmno, Belzec, Majdanek, Sobibor, and Treblinka—as well as lesser-known camps in Warsaw, Janowska, and Belarus. The most com- mon methods for the "efficient" killing of inmates were gas chambers, mass shootings, starvation, and torture. Buchenwald, on the other hand, was a concentration camp located in central Germany that was used pri- marily for forced labor. The majority of inmates were political prisoners. Death rates were exceptionally high from malnourishment, disease, and human experimentation. In 1933 the Nazis built Dachau outside of Munich as a model for future concentration camps. It housed political prisoners and Jews. Most of the 25,000 deaths there were caused by disease, malnu- trition, and suicide.

Barring the Door

There was no way for the Allied nations to know how far Hitler's anti- Jewish passions might go. But the closing of U.S., British, and other

European borders to desperate Jewish immigrants signaled to Hitler that other Western nations cared little for the plight of the Jews and that his strategy for their permanent elimination would not be met with major repercussions. Hitler's propaganda minister, Joseph Goebbels, noted in a December 13, 1942, diary entry:

> The question of Jewish persecution in Europe is being given top news priority by the English and the Americans. . . . At bottom, however, I believe both the English and the Americans are happy that we are exterminating the Jewish riff-raff.[16]

James Carroll, author of *Constantine's Sword: the Church and the Jews*, has researched the history of anti-Semitism in Europe. He wrote: "Crucial to [the Final Solution] building to a point of no return was Hitler's discovery of the political indifference of the democracies to the fate of the Jews."[17]

In June 1940, Assistant Secretary of State Breckinridge Long, fearing that Jews would become spies and saboteurs, urged foreign consuls to use any means necessary to frustrate Jewish sanctuary. He even sent a memorandum to U.S. embassy officials in Europe suggesting ways of obstructing the issuance of visas to Jewish escapees from Nazi Germany. Long wrote:

> We can delay and effectively stop for a temporary period of indefinite length the number of immigrants into the United States. We could do this by simply advising our consuls to put every obstacle in the way and to require additional evidence and to resort to various administrative devices which would postpone and postpone and postpone the granting of the visas.[18]

The affect of the Breckinridge Long memo was immediate. Margaret E. Jones, an American Quaker working with European Jewish refugees, complained of the bureaucratic maze that had been thrown up to stop Jews from getting visas. She wrote:

> We cannot continue to let these tragic people go on hoping that if they comply with every requirement, if they get all the special documents required (Marks are increasingly needed by the Jews just to live), if they nerve themselves for the final interview at the Consulate, they

may just possibly be the lucky ones to get visas when we know that practically no one is granted visas in Germany today. As thee knows, the whole question of affidavits is involved—irrevocable trust funds as required by the Consulate—we can't go out to individuals in this country for this basic cooperation when we know that regardless of what we or the applicant does, he is not going to get the visa.[19]

Even though U.S. immigration law allowed for the annual admission of 150,000 immigrants, a year after the extent of the Nazi extermination campaign against the Jews was known, the United States had only allowed 4,705 Jews fleeing Nazi persecution into the country.[20]

Many Americans were fearful that their country could become a dumping ground for persecuted Jewish minorities, who might be subversives as well. But such anti-immigration sentiments had not begun with the question of letting the Jews into the United States. As early as the Irish immigration of the mid-nineteenth century, opposition to immigration of the "wrong" kind had developed as a powerful theme in U.S. history. The Immigration Act of 1924 reflected these biases in the national origins quota system that limited the number of foreign-born persons in the United States to 2 percent of the American population of that particular origin. The act also barred immigrants from Japan, China, and other Asian countries.

Mrs. Agnes Waters testified before a congressional committee debating a bill to allow refugee children into the United States. She warned that passage of the legislation would bring to American shores "thousands of motherless, embittered, persecuted children of undesirable foreigners," who might themselves become "potential leaders of a revolt against our American form of government."[21]

In July 1941 an article entitled "State Department Appeasers" appeared in *The New Republic* that called American diplomats like Breckinridge Long; James B. Stewart, the American consul in Zurich; and Leland B. Morris, the American consul in Berlin, "exclusionists" and criticized them for harboring strong anti-immigrationist sentiments.

Feigned Skepticism

In early August 1942 the secretary of the World Jewish Congress in Switzerland, Gerhart Riegner, secretly transmitted through the British Foreign Office a report that signaled Hitler's intention to exterminate all

European Jews. Riegner had obtained this information from a German industrialist who traveled in top Nazi circles. Six months before, U.S. intelligence had intercepted a report from a Chilean diplomat named Gonzalo Montt Rivas based in Prague, Czechoslovakia. He informed his government that Hitler intended to "eradicate all the Jews."[22] State Department officials summarizing the dispatch for the Office of Strategic Services (OSS) called Riegner's message "a wild rumor inspired by Jewish fears."[23] By November of that year, the State Department had received documentary evidence confirming not only earlier reports, but also the fact that Hitler had already murdered two million Jews. The *New York Times* buried the story on page ten.[24]

The State Department was even more cryptic, fearing that if reports of genocide against the Jews became known, Americans might become more anti-Semitic and less supportive of the war effort as a conflict affecting more than just the Jewish people. Given the political realities, it became convenient for American and other Western officials to express skepticism over the reports. Victor Cavendish-Bentinck of the British Foreign Office wrote in an August 27, 1942, memorandum responding to reports of genocide, that "the Poles and to a greater extent the Jews, tend to exaggerate German atrocities in order to stoke us up."[25]

The Bermuda Conference

In April 1943, the United States and Britain convened a closed-door conference in Bermuda to discuss the situation of Jewish refugees escaping from the Nazis. The conference accomplished little because the American delegates were restricted by the provisions of a secret directive, which declared among other things:

> There is no indication that the Congress would be likely to act favorably upon any proposal that the immigration laws be relaxed or suspended in behalf of refugees. In a previous Congress a Joint Resolution to authorize the admission of 20,000 German children failed of passage. Several bills to make the unused portions of the immigration quotas available to refugees without regard to the national origins principle embodied in our quota system have met with no success. Other legislation to relax the immigration laws has been proposed from time to time but has not been enacted.[26]

Jewish leaders submitted a plan of rescue to the Bermuda Conference. It read:

> We would be less than frank if we did not convey to you the anguish of the Jewish community of this country over the failure of the United Nations to act until now to rescue the Jews of Europe. For many months it has been authenticated that the Nazis have marked the Jewish population of Europe for total extermination and that it is estimated that almost three million Jews have been done to death, while a similar fate awaits those who remain. World civilization has been stirred to its depths by these horrors. Every section of public opinion throughout the world, and more particularly in England and in the United States, has spoken out in the demand that the United Nations act before it is too late to save those who can still be saved. Six months have elapsed, however, and no action has as yet been taken. In the meantime it is reported that thousands of Jews continue to be murdered daily.[27]

But the pleas of Jewish leaders were ignored.

Acquiescence to Murder

In September 1943 a bill was introduced into Congress allowing refugees to enter the United States temporarily. It died in committee. In early 1943 the World Jewish Congress had attempted to wire money to Europe to ransom Jewish refugees fleeing Nazi death camps in France and Romania. All such international transactions had to be approved by the U.S. Treasury Department. Josiah E. DuBois, a thirty-year-old attorney in the Foreign Funds Control, a unit of the Treasury, became involved in trying to figure out why the transaction had been held up for months. The deeper he dug, the angrier he got. Finally, in 1943 on Christmas Day the young Protestant who had no particular ties to the Jewish community wrote an angry report to Secretary of the Treasury Henry Morgenthau, Jr., entitled "Report to the Secretary on the Acquiescence of this Government in the Murder of the Jews." It was dated January 13, 1944, and among other things declared:

> Since the time when this government knew that the Jews were being murdered, our State Department has failed to take any positive steps reasonably calculated to save any of these people. Although State has

used the device of setting up intergovernmental organizations to survey the whole refugee problem, and calling conferences such as the Bermuda Conference to explore the whole refugee problem, making it appear that positive action could be expected, in fact nothing has been accomplished. . . . Probably in all 5,703 years, Jews have hardly had a time as tragic and hopeless as the one which they are undergoing now. One of the most tragic factors about the situation is that while singled out for suffering and martyrdom by their enemies, they seem to have been forgotten by the nations which claim to fight for the cause of humanity. WE should remember the Jewish slaughterhouse of Europe and ask what is being done—and I emphasize the word "done"—to get some of these suffering human beings out of the slaughter while yet alive.[28]

Not only were the Allies restrained from accepting Jews fleeing Nazi persecution before the war, their military commanders also refused to bomb railway lines during World War II, which led to clearly demarcated concentration camps.[29] A heated debate has erupted among historians and Holocaust survivors as to whether this decision might have been motivated by anti-Semitism. Professor David Wyman of the University of Massachusetts posed the question:

How could it be that the governments of the two great Western democracies knew that a place existed where 2,000 helpless human beings could be killed every 30 minutes, knew that such killings actually did occur over and over again, and yet did not feel driven to search for some way to wipe such a scourge from the earth?[30]

In March 1941 British Intelligence began receiving reports from a Polish Army spy, Capt. Witold Pilecki, who had allowed himself to be imprisoned at Auschwitz in order to gather intelligence and foment revolt. His detailed reports confirmed the mass executions at the camp. Professor Hamerow has suggested, for example, that the Allies had one overriding fear. Should the Germans turn away from the Jewish extermination campaign on account of Allied bombing of such facilities, the alternative might have been even more unpalatable to the West. Hamerow asked:

What would happen if the Germans suddenly opened the gates and the Allies had to face a deluge of impoverished, hungry, sick refugees? Should they admit them and risk aggravating ethnic prejudice at home? Or should they exclude them, to the grim satisfaction of the Hitler government, which had always accused its enemies of shedding crocodile tears?[31]

But it is also true that war has its own logic and anything not making a direct military contribution to the war is a tough sell to the military. The war's unquestionable goal was to defeat Hitler, and World War II military strategists concluded that bombing anything other than a military target was not going to contribute to that goal.

In January 1944, after Secretary Morgenthau and U.S. Jewish groups began to apply intense pressure on President Roosevelt, he established the War Refugee Board (WRB). In a press release announcing creation of the agency, the President stated that "it was urgent that action be taken at once to forestall the plan of the Nazis to exterminate all the Jews and other persecuted minorities in Europe."[32] The WRB coordinated its efforts with the American Jewish Joint Distribution Committee, the World Jewish Congress, and resistance organizations in Nazi-occupied territories. Their combined efforts succeeded in rescuing 200,000 Jews from Nazi-occupied territories. But it was too little, too late for the six million Jews who perished in Nazi gas chambers.

2

Rescue

Despite the horrors of the Holocaust and the pangs of guilt the West felt on account of it, none of these nations was in a position to open its borders to massive Jewish immigration. The lock out that had preceded World War II was still firmly in place after the war. A quarter of a million Jews emerged from concentration camps and hiding. They were malnourished, diseased, and emotionally numbed by the genocide they had somehow survived. As they languished in displaced persons' camps in Germany, Austria, and Italy, the question became who will offer a home to these displaced people? The answer was no one.

In August 1945 the newly elected President Harry S. Truman suggested in a letter to Clement Attlee, the British prime minister, that 100,000 visas be issued for Jews to immigrate to Palestine. The British government, straining to protect its Arab alliances in the Middle East, issued a statement in the House of Commons saying that it rejected the view that " Jews should be driven out of Europe or that they should not be permitted to live again in these countries without discrimination, contributing their ability and talent toward rebuilding the prosperity of Europe."[1]

President Truman had also commissioned Earl G. Harrison, dean of the University of Pennsylvania Law School and former commissioner of

Immigration to investigate charges of abuse of Jewish displaced persons in European resettlement camps. Harrison issued a preliminary report on August 3, 1945, declaring:

1. Generally speaking, three months after V-E Day and even longer after the liberation of individual groups, many Jewish displaced persons and other possibly non-repatriables are living under guard behind barbed-wire fences, in camps of several descriptions (built by the Germans for slave-laborers and Jews), including some of the most notorious of the concentration camps, amidst crowded, frequently unsanitary and generally grim conditions, in complete idleness, with no opportunity, except surreptitiously, to communicate with the outside world, waiting, hoping for some word of encouragement and action in their behalf.

2. While there has been marked improvement in the health of survivors of the Nazi starvation and persecution program, there are many pathetic malnutrition cases both among the hospitalized and in the general population of the camps. The death rate has been high since liberation, as was to be expected. One Army Chaplain, a Rabbi, personally attended, since liberation 23,000 burials (90 percent Jews) at Bergen Belsen alone, one of the largest and most vicious of the concentration camps, where, incidentally, despite persistent reports to the contrary, fourteen thousand displaced persons are still living, including over seven thousand Jews. At many of the camps and centers including those where serious starvation cases are, there is a marked and serious lack of needed medical supplies.[2]

Blocking Jewish Immigration

Despite the noble sentiments expressed by the British, they continued to bar Jewish emigration from their own shores. Truman was, likewise, unable to get Congress to open U.S. borders to Jewish immigration. On December 22, 1945, he issued an executive order called the Truman Directive. It authorized that priority be given within the quota system to displaced persons, even though fewer than 16,000 Jewish displaced persons, including 1,387 orphaned children, gained entry into the United States.

However, in 1948 Congress passed bold new immigration laws that allowed 80,000 Jews into the country. This legislation can be seen as a major turning point in American public views toward immigration. But by then, most European Jews had died in the Holocaust, and survivors had given up hope of being accepted into a Western country and allowed themselves to be shipped off to the fledgling state of Israel.

The situation for refugees fleeing the Nazis had been equally dismal in other Western nations. Between 1933 and 1945, Canada had only allowed 5,000 Jews into the country. Professor Hamerow observed: "Canada never pretended to be ready to embrace the 'huddled masses' or the 'wretched refuse' from the other side of the ocean."[3] It was only after the war that it liberalized its immigration policy and allowed roughly 40,000 Holocaust survivors to settle within its borders. As for Australia, Professor Suzanne Rutland wrote:

> In the face of hostile public reactions to Jewish refugee migration, the government sought to minimise the number of Jewish migrants permitted into Australia. A series of bureaucratic measures were introduced to limit the number of Jewish immigrants, but the government denied any form of discrimination when questioned by the established Jewish community leadership.[4]

Growing Arab Fears

After World War II, the world knew what Jews had suffered at the hands of European anti-Semitism. Yet the best the West could offer the survivors of the Nazi gas chambers was the hope of being smuggled into a British colony in the Middle East, populated by resentful and riotous Arabs.

Palestine had come under British control after World War I through a League of Nations mandate. In 1917 British foreign minister Arthur Balfour sent a letter to Lord Walter Rothschild, stating that the British government viewed "with favour the establishment in Palestine of a national home for the Jewish people." But it also went on to warn, "nothing shall be done which may prejudice the civil and religious rights of existing non-Jewish communities in Palestine."

Early Zionists used this policy statement to support Jewish immigration to Palestine. But as growing numbers of Jews poured into the country, the Arabs reacted with fear and anger. On April 4, 1920, Palestinians who had congregated in the Jerusalem city square to celebrate the annual Nabi Musa spring festival began attacking Jews in the Old City's alleys. Five

Jews and four Arabs were killed. The following year, on the eve of a May Day parade, the Jewish Communist Party of Palestine began distributing flyers in Yiddish and Arabic calling for the overthrow of British rule and establishment of a Soviet Palestine. The next day, a fight broke out between the Jewish Communist Party and a rival Jewish organization. Rumors began to spread that Arabs were being attacked. Rioting broke out and left 47 Jews and 48 Arabs dead. In November 1920 fighting erupted between Arabs and Jews in Jerusalem once again.

In August 1929 an incident that came to be known as the Hebron massacre took place. Arabs, who were incited by a false rumor that Jews had seized the Muslim holy places and were killing Arabs, killed sixty-seven Jews. By 1936 Palestinian resentment to continued Jewish immigration had become so intense that a general strike was called in April of that year. Arabs attacked Jewish settlements and the railway line leading to Haifa. Even though the strike was called off in October, violence between the Arabs and Jews continued to escalate. Within three years, 5,000 Arabs, 400 Jews, and 200 British soldiers had been killed.

The Great Arab Revolt
In April 1936 a spontaneous Arab uprising against the growing number of Jewish settlers erupted in Jaffa. Israeli professors Baruch Kimmerling and Joel S. Migdal in *The Palestinian People: A History* described the event as follows:

> As the first sustained violent uprising of the Palestinian national movement, and the first major episode of this sort since 1834, perhaps no event has been more momentous in Palestinian history than the Great Arab Revolt. It mobilized thousands of Arabs from every stratum of society, all over the country, heralding the emergence of a national movement in ways that isolated incidents and formal delegations simply could not accomplish. It also provoked unprecedented counter mobilization. . . . The Zionists embarked upon a militarization of their own national movement—nearly 15,000 Jews were under arms by the Revolt's end. . . .[5]

After the revolt subsided in March 1939, the British government set up the Peel Commission, headed by Lord Earl Peel, to investigate the causes of the uprising and to make recommendations for policy changes in the way the British Mandate of Palestine was being administered. The Peel Commission issued a report identifying two underlying causes for this outbreak of violence: "1. The desire of the Arabs for national independence; 2. Their hatred and fear of the establishment of the Jewish National Home."[6] The commission also proposed the partitioning of Palestine into two states—one Jewish, the other Arab. Arab leaders rejected the proposals while the Jewish community found itself split on the matter. The British government set up the Woodhead Commission to examine the findings of the Peel Commission. The Woodhead Report declared that the partition plan proposed by the previous commission was unworkable.

British and Jewish Confrontation in Palestine
During this period, Jewish settlers faced more than growing Palestinian resentment and violence. They also found themselves battling the British, who from the beginning of World War II had started reducing the number of Jewish refugees allowed into Palestine. After the quota of 15,000 immigrants was met, Jews heading for Palestine were rerouted to Mauritius or placed in British detention camps. As Zionist groups became more desperate, their actions became more violent. On November 6, 1944, a Zionist paramilitary group called Lehi, an acronym for *Lohamei Herut Israel* (Fighters for the Freedom of Israel), assassinated the top British diplomat in the Middle East, Lord Walter Guinness Moyne, who had been an outspoken critic of resettling Jews in Palestine. Yaakov Banai, a Lehi military commander, later identified three reasons for the group's decision to assassinate Lord Moyne:

1. To show the world that this conflict wasn't between a government and its citizens like Britain tried to show but between citizens and a foreign rule.
2. To prove that the conflict was between the Jewish People and the British Imperialism.
3. To take the "War of Liberation" out of the Land of Israel and the Yishuv. The trial wasn't planned but the action had to capture a place in the world press and lead political thoughts.[7]

Scapegoating Zionism

The aftermath of World War II became political Zionism's defining moment. After the discovery of the atrocities committed against the Jews, who could argue that this long-suffering community did not deserve a safe haven, a homeland? International sympathy for Zionism swelled except, of course, among the enraged people whose lands were being expropriated for that purpose.

It is true that Zionist leaders had an agenda—to populate Palestine with as many Jews as possible. But Zionist idealism, aimed at shipping Holocaust survivors to the politically unstable Middle East, became a convenient excuse used by Western nations, which for political and economic reasons, found themselves unable to open their own borders to Jewish refugees. For instance, at the end of World War II, one of the proposals on the table, according to Israeli professor Zeev Tzahor, was the establishment of "a limited autonomy on German soil so as to constitute a solution for several tens of thousands of Jews."[8] Professor Tzahor identified other proposals as well, which included "dividing up of the Jews among the various European countries, and massive migration to the United States."[9]

However, the West lacked the political will to act on any of these proposals. Thus, the Zionists seized the moment. Professor Tzahor explained: "During the summer of 1945 more than 150 emissaries from Palestine reached these camps," and they envisaged the refugees as the "spearhead of the Zionist struggle."[10] By February 1947, when the second Congress of the Liberated Jews in the U.S.-occupied zone of Germany met, it had become "political suicide" to advocate any proposals other than immigration to Palestine.[11]

The Survivors' Dilemma

The Zionists had, before World War II, attracted a marginal following as they competed with other intellectual and ideological currents among European Jewry. But they seized the opportunity created by the Holocaust to win adherents to their cause. There were certainly biblical merits to rebuilding a homeland lost 2,000 years ago. Even so, most Jewish survivors of World War II would have chosen to settle in the United States or Europe. Israeli professor Ilan Pappé explained:

In 1947 the U.N. appointed a special body, the United Nations Special Committee on Palestine (UNSCOP), to make the decision over Palestine. UNSCOP members were asked to visit the camps of Holocaust survivors. Many of these survivors wanted to emigrate to the United States, a wish that undermined the Zionist claims that the fate of European Jewry was connected to that of the Jewish community in Palestine. When UNSCOP representatives arrived at the camps, they were unaware that backstage manipulations were limiting their contacts solely to survivors who wished to emigrate to Palestine.[12]

One worker employed by the Jewish Agency even wrote home to his girlfriend: "We have to change our style and handwriting constantly so that they will think that the questionnaires were filled in by the refugees."[13]

Morris Ernst, a Jewish attorney and friend of the late president Roosevelt, observed:

> What if Canada, Australia, South America, England, and the United States were all to open a door to some migration? Even today [written in 1947] it is my judgment, and I have been in Germany since the war, that only a minority of the Jewish DP's [displaced persons] would choose Palestine.[14]

However, as their time in these camps passed from months to years, Holocaust survivors saw the reality of the situation all too clearly. If no Western nation would open its doors to these destitute, emotionally scarred refugees, then embracing Zionism and trying to make their way to Palestine were their only choices.

Euro-Zionism

Sadly, the Zionists, blinded both by idealism and desperation, had no idea what they were getting themselves and millions of their co-religionists into by attempting to establish a safe haven for persecuted Jews in Palestine. Political Zionism was a European intellectual movement, developed and led by European Jews in response to European anti-Semitism.

In 1905 alone there were pogroms in 660 different places in Russia, and more than 800 Jews were killed—all this in a period of less than two weeks. Two years before, an anti-Semitic hoax in the form of a tract called

The Protocols of the Elders of Zion first emerged in Russia. The document purported to describe a secret plot organized by a cabal of rabbis to control the world. Its 24 Protocols, or Instructions, intended to foment violence and hatred against Jews, claimed that Jews were instigating world wars, economic depressions, and a global brainwashing campaign in addition to other nefarious acts. This was the reality of life for many of Europe's Jews.

Many intellectual currents vied for supremacy among world Jewry. But they died in Hitler's death camps with most of European Jewry. As for the Zionist movement, the Sephardim and Mizrahim—the Oriental and Arab Jews from Middle Eastern countries—had been excluded from leadership positions. This exclusion was deliberate. Its Ashkenazic, or European, Jewish leaders disparaged or expressed open contempt for this non-European element of the Jewish community. Zionist leader David Ben-Gurion once commented: "We do not want Israelis to become Arabs. We are in duty bound to fight against the spirit of the Levant, which corrupts individuals and societies, and preserve authentic Jewish values."[15] Abba Eban, who was to become Israel's foreign minister from 1966 to 1974, declared similarly: "One of the great apprehensions which afflict us is the danger of the predominance of immigrants of Oriental origin forcing Israel to equalize its cultural level with that of the neighboring world."[16] The attitude of early Zionists toward Middle Eastern and African Jews was not appreciably different from the way they viewed the Palestinians.

Without any high-level input from Middle Eastern Jews, the Euro-Zionists knew little about the country they now called home. Israel's founder and first prime minister spoke at least six languages, but Arabic was not one of them. Nor did other Zionist leaders have or cultivate familiarity with the culture and language of their new neighborhood. This is so even though Hebrew and Arabic are both Semitic languages and are similar in vocabulary and structure.[17] The Zionists misunderstood the demography of the region and its history and knew nothing about the Islamic religion. Nor did they understand the dynamics of Middle Eastern politics. What to them may have appeared to be "undifferentiated Arabs" had, by the early twentieth century, already evolved into the roiling nationalisms of Palestinians, Egyptians, Syrians, and others, as meaningful in distinction as the differences British, Americans, and South Africans feel toward one another, even though they share a common language. Most important, the

Zionists ignored Arab grievances, especially their deepest yearnings to throw off the yoke of colonialism in order to establish their own independent states.

Even though Europeans had engaged in relentless persecution against their Jewish communities for millennia, the deeper tragedy was that these Jews had become acculturated into those Western cultures. It may not have been obvious except when they were thrust into the non-European environments of the Middle East. Early Zionists, like most Europeans, looked upon the Palestinians as primitive, almost aboriginal people. Jewish leaders assumed that they would vanish when pressed into the sieve of the larger Arab world.

There were exceptions, men of prescience such as Asher Zvi Ginsberg (1856–1927). A Zionist essayist and political thinker, Ginsberg wrote under the pen name Ahad Ha'am. He was responsible for reviving the Hebrew language when others, like founder of political Zionism Theodore Herzl, believed that German should be the language of the Jewish homeland. In 1891 Ha'am declared:

> From abroad we are accustomed to believing that the Arabs are all desert savages, like donkeys, who neither see nor understand what goes on around them. But this is a big mistake. . . . The Arabs, and especially those in the cities, understand our deeds and our desires in Eretz Israel, but they keep quiet and pretend not to understand, since they do not see our present activities as a threat to their future. . . . However, if the time comes when the life of our people in Eretz Israel develops to the point of encroaching upon the native population, they will not easily yield their place.[18]

Ha'am's cultural voice was drowned out by Herzl's more activist political wing of the Zionist movement. University of Calgary professor of Israel studies, Dr. Alan Dowty, has pointed out that early Zionists like Menachem Ussishkin, Leon Motzkin, Ber Borochov, and Theodor Herzl "tended to minimize [Arab hostility] as a long-term threat and to express confidence that economic prosperity brought by Zionism, together with fair treatment of Arabs *as individuals,* would eliminate the problem by integrating the Arab populace into a modern democratic (and Jewish) society."[19]

The Exodus

With legal immigration blocked by the British, the Zionists' main preoccupation was how to smuggle increasing numbers of Jews into Palestine rather than how to placate restive Arabs. After World War II, Zionist efforts to resettle Holocaust survivors became even more aggressive and desperate. Aliyah Bet was the code name given to the clandestine operation of resettling Jews in the Middle East. In 1945 the Zionists set up an underground network called Bricha (Hebrew for "escape"), charged with getting Jewish refugees from Europe to Palestine. The Mossad—the Jewish intelligence agency responsible for helping Bricha ships run the British blockade—aided this operation. Between 1945 and 1948, approximately 70,000 Jewish refugees escaped Europe through this operation. However, the British apprehended about 85 percent of them and most of them were deported to internment camps in Cyprus, which was also an English colony at the time.[20]

Zionist frustrations exploded to the surface. In July 1946, members of the Jewish paramilitary group, Irgun, blew up the King David Hotel in Jerusalem in an attempt to pressure Great Britain into allowing Holocaust refugees into Palestine. It was the headquarters of the British administration in Palestine. Irgun's leader, Menachem Begin, insisted that he had sent a warning but that British officials had ignored it. The attack killed 92 people.

The British retaliated by commandeering even more Zionist ships bound for Palestine. The most high-profile case occurred in the summer of 1947. The *Exodus 1947* had sailed from a port near the city of Marseilles, France, carrying 4,515 Jewish passengers. When it made its way to within twenty nautical miles of the Palestine coast, the British navy apprehended the ship. In the ensuing skirmish, one sailor was killed and several others injured. The ship's Jewish passengers were returned to France.

3

Trapped

By the winter of 1947 a severe economic crisis hit Great Britain and the country could no longer allocate the military resources needed to administer and patrol its volatile Mandate in Palestine. Violence between Jews and Arabs and attacks on British troops were escalating. London also could not afford the diplomatic strains on its relationship with the United States and other Western allies that had been caused by its refusal to grant 100,000 Jews entry into Palestine. This British intransigence embarrassed the Allies, which had no desire to settle Holocaust survivors within their own national borders.

At a conference in London in late January 1947, both the Arabs and Zionists rejected a plan put forth by the British that called for a five-year trusteeship, allowing for the immigration of 96,000 Jews and the establishment of an independent state with an Arab majority. Shortly thereafter, the British government decided to wash its hands of the problem of Palestine by terminating the Mandate and turning the territory over to the United Nations.

On November 29, 1947, the UN General Assembly agreed to partition Palestine between Arabs and Jews with a two-thirds vote, with Britain and nine other countries abstaining. Avraham Burg, an Israeli intellectual and former speaker of the Israeli Knesset, in interpreting that vote, asserted, "Without the Shoah [Holocaust] United Nations resolutions that brought about the establishment of Israel would not have been passed. Neither would the immediate international recognition of the new state have been granted. . . ."[1]

Most Jews celebrated, now seeing Zionism as their only option for survival. But some, like Menachem Begin, the head of the paramilitary group Irgun, believed that it was not enough, declaring, "The partition of the homeland is illegal. . . . The Land of Israel will be restored to the people of Israel. All of it. And for ever."[2]

The Palestinians and the neighboring Arab states rejected the partition plan but lacked political clout in the international arena to give voice to their disappointment. Civil war broke out between Jews and Arabs in Palestine. During the winter of 1948, violence had escalated to more than 100 deaths and 200 casualties per week. The Jewish population was under strict orders to hold all territories under its control while Palestinian civilians fled from zones of fighting. When soldiers from the Irgun and Lehi paramilitary groups massacred 100 Arabs at Deir Yassan, thousands more Palestinians left their homes in terror.

Plan D

On May 14, 1948, one day before the expiration of the British Mandate of Palestine, David Ben-Gurion declared Israel to be an independent nation. The United States, the Soviet Union, and other Western nations recognized it immediately. The Arab states of Egypt and Jordan launched an invasion, but the Zionists were ready. In fact, as Professor Avi Shlaim, an Iraqi Jew and dual citizen of Great Britain and Israel, pointed out in *The Iron Wall*, a strategy had been defined decades ago by the Zionist leader Ze'ev Jabotinsky. In two 1923 articles Ze'ev Jabotinsky outlined a plan in which the Jews would establish an "iron wall" around Palestine, taking the offensive against the Arabs and eventually beating them into submission.[3] Every military confrontation between Jews and Arabs would feed into that trajectory.

All Jewish men and women older than fourteen received mandatory military training during this period. Thus, the Haganah was able to supply 35,000 troops to the new Israel Defense Forces (IDF). The militant offshoots of Haganah, another paramilitary group called the Stern Gang, and

Irgun provided an additional 3,000 troops with several thousand more coming from the ranks of armed settlers.[4] Unlike the Jewish community, the Palestinians had no organized army at the start of the war. The newly formed Arab League recruited volunteers from Lebanon, Syria, Iraq, and Egypt, creating an invasion force of 21,000 soldiers.

The official version of Israel's founding claimed that Arab leaders on radio broadcasts had urged the Palestinians to flee so as not to be caught in the cross fire of their armies' confrontation with the Israel Defense Force. But the truth was more multifaceted. Recently declassified material showed ". . . not only explicit expulsion orders, but also evidence of war crimes committed by Israeli soldiers, including murder, torture, rape, and looting," Tom Segev wrote in *Elvis in Jerusalem*.[5]

Gen. Yigael Yadin, head of the Operations Branch of Israeli forces, devised Plan D, which was launched two months before Israel's 1948 declaration of independence. The plan stipulated:

> the destruction of villages (by fire, blowing up and mining)—especially of those villages over which we cannot gain [permanent] control. Gaining of control will be accomplished in accordance with the following instructions: the encircling of the village and the search of it. In the event of resistance—the destruction of the resisting forces and the expulsion of the population beyond the boundaries of the State.[6]

Plan D succeeded in cleansing much of the territory granted to the Palestinians under the UN partition agreement of its Arab inhabitants. In short, as Israeli professor and historian Benny Morris explained:

> . . . the refugee problem was caused by attacks by Jewish forces on Arab villages and towns and by the inhabitants' fear of such attacks, compounded by expulsions, atrocities, and rumour of atrocities—and by the crucial Israeli Cabinet decision in June 1948 to bar a refugee return.[7]

Like generals fighting their last war, the Israelis saw in their new Arab enemies the demonic face of Adolf Hitler while their Palestinian adversaries saw in them the ferocious new face of an old foe—European colonialism. Also, the historical timing for the creation of a Jewish state in the Islamic Middle East could not have been worse. Not only did Western countries back Israel, but 90 percent of the founding population of Jews came from Europe. Having just thrown off the embittering yoke of European colonialism, the Arabs saw a new European colony being created in their midst. The post–World War II era was also a time when white settler colonies were being dismantled throughout the third world. While on one hand Israelis justified their Middle East presence in terms of biblical claims, on the other they touted Israel to their Western allies as an enclave of European democracy and sanity in the midst of the alien Arab world.

By the time an armistice agreement was signed on July 20, 1949, the Jews controlled 50 percent more territory than the UN Partition Plan had originally allotted for them. An estimated 711,000 Palestinians had been displaced outside of Israel with new laws in place that would not allow them to return to their homes.

The Language of Force

The Israelis also might have drawn a dangerously false lesson from their victory. Nahum Goldmann, president of the World Zionist Congress, wrote in his autobiography:

> . . . The [1948 war] victory offered such a glorious contrast to the centuries of persecution and humiliation, of adaptation and compromise, that it seemed to indicate the only direction that could possibly be taken from then on. To brook through nothing, tolerate no attack, but cut through Gordian knots, and to shape history by creating facts seemed so simple, so compelling, so satisfying that it became Israel's policy in its conflict with the Arab world.[8]

Professor Avi Shlaim has researched the tensions that arose between the militant leaders of early Israel, like Ben-Gurion, and their moderate opponents, the faction led by future prime minister Moshe Sharett. According to Shlaim, the IDF inherited the militant viewpoint, arguing that Arabs "only understood the language of force"—that is, the belief that the militarily stronger side will dominate the political landscape and that Arabs would perceive of any compromise on the part of Jews as a sign of weakness.[9] Shaim also asserted:

The moderates did not object to military retaliation in principle, but they wanted to use it in a more selective and controlled way and only after careful consideration of the likely political consequences. They were more sensitive to Arab feelings and to world opinion; they wanted to create a climate that would favor the possibilities of peaceful coexistence in the Middle East; they feared that frequent and excessive use of force would further inflame Arab hatred of Israel and set back the prospects of reconciliation.[10]

Since warfare is ubiquitous to human history, at some time or another, all societies have justified belligerent actions by accusing their enemies of "only understanding the language of force."

The Six-Day War

With fortitude and a devotion born of necessity, the Israelis went about the business of building a Jewish homeland. Within a short time they had accomplished the near impossible: creating a viable first world economy; reviving a dormant language, which had for 2,000 years been used solely for liturgical purposes; developing a full-fledged democracy; absorbing immigrants from more than a hundred different countries; and becoming a pioneer in both agricultural development and high technology. But they could not bring peace and security to Holocaust survivors and other citizens of their Jewish state.

In May 1967 Egypt expelled UN troops overseeing the demilitarization of Sinai, deployed 100,000 soldiers on its border with Israel, and blockaded the Straits of Tiran to Israeli shipping. Fearing an invasion, the IDF launched a preemptive attack on June 5, 1967, destroying nearly simultaneously the air forces of Egypt, Jordan, Syria, and Iraq. By the time a cease-fire agreement was signed on June 10, Israel had gained control of the Gaza Strip and Sinai Peninsula from Egypt; the West Bank of the Jordan River, including East Jerusalem from Jordan; and the Syrian Golan Heights. Israelis were euphoric. Ze'ev Jabotinsky's iron wall strategy of building a Jewish state, legitimized through military might, seemed to be working.

The Six-Day War also reinforced the military ethos of the Jewish people, who had suffered not only the loss of millions of lives during World War II, but also a deep sense of shame at the inability of their community to fight back against the Nazis. Zionism rejected anything that smacked of pacifistic diaspora-Jewish behavior. Sabras, Israeli-born Jews, were known to refer to Holocaust survivors as *sabon* (soap). Journalist Anton La Guardia explained that it derived from the false rumor that "the Nazis had made soap from the bodies of Jews because of a shortage of industrial fats, and sums up in a single word the contempt that sabras felt for Jews who did not live up to the heroic ideal."[10] In its stead, the sabra presented an invigorating image of the handsome Jewish warrior, enwrapped in valor, armed to the teeth and ruthless if need be, to save his people from harm.

However, when the euphoria died down, a new dilemma began to take shape. What was Israel to do with the territories it had just seized, given the fact that several million angry Arabs inhabited them? Israelis prided themselves on being the only functional democracy in the Middle East so another problem was how to exercise democratic principles while maintaining its Jewish character and dominance. The Israelis conferred the opportunity for full citizenship on the inhabitants of East Jerusalem and the Golan Heights, although most of its residents, in an act of protest, have refused to apply for it. But the larger Arab populations of the West Bank and Gaza remained in political limbo.

In November 1967 the UN Security Council passed Resolution 242, which called on Israel to withdraw from all Occupied Territories in exchange for peace treaties with its Arab neighbors. Many diplomatic initiatives have been undertaken over the decades since its passage, but the resolution has never been implemented.

Despite the environment of hostilities, Israel developed into a richly layered democracy. But, not surprisingly, militarization came to dominate the cultural landscape since permanent mobilization for war was a necessary component for survival of the Jewish state. Professor Uri Ben-Eliezer of the University of Haifa has suggested in *The Making of Israeli Militarism* that Zionism structured itself in the form of a colonial enterprise from the beginning. It allied itself with the big European powers and convinced itself that the Palestinian issue would be fixed in time by the Jewish state's insurmountable military power. The predictably hostile Arab response to the situation became Israel's excuse for maintaining a militaristic culture.[12]

The Curse of Unintended Consequences
The humiliating defeat of the Egyptian, Syrian, and Jordanian armies by

the Israelis during the Six-Day War weakened the hold of Arab nationalism as a rallying cry in the region. But rather than auguring to Israel's benefit, this new development bolstered a movement—Islamic fundamentalism—that had, until that moment, subsisted at the margins of Middle East life. The *New York Times* reported:

> Many people feel that the resurgence of Islamic militancy in Egypt dates to that overwhelming defeat . . . everyone was questioning themselves after the war . . . they kept asking what it was about our society, our culture, our political system that could pave the way for such a defeat.[13]

The answer supplied by militant Muslim fundamentalists was that the community had strayed too far from the dictates of the *Shari'a*, Islamic religious law. Professor of international relations Bassam Tibi concluded: "The Arab defeat in the Six-Day War of 1967 had been one of the major factors underlying the politicization of religion."[14] Adding to the Arabs' sense of shame was the fact that during that brief war, the Israelis had captured East Jerusalem and asserted control over the entire city, including many Muslim holy sites.

As Zachary Karabell explained in Columbia University Professor Richard Bulliet's *Columbia History of the Twentieth Century*:

> In the 1980s and into the 1990s, fundamentalist groups became prominent in most countries in the Islamic world. . . . In Sudan, a military-fundamentalist alliance resulted in the most radical Islamic state besides Iran. In Saudi Arabia, the puritanical Wahhabi sect, which had been subservient to the Saudi monarchy since the 1920s, gained renewed strength as Saudi oil revenues stagnated and the lavish, un-Islamic lifestyles of the Saudi royalty became more widely known. In Egypt and Jordan, the Muslim Brotherhood was and still is the leading opposition group to the government, while in Israel and the Occupied Territories, Hamas and several smaller groups speak in the name of Islam to fight any Arab reconciliation with the Israelis.[15]

War and Peace

On October 6, 1973, six years and four months after the previous Middle East war, Egypt and Syria launched a joint attack against Israel on Yom

Kippur, the Jewish holiday of atonement. The Arabs had learned a few lessons from their previous defeat and came on strong in the first two days of fighting. The United States and Soviet Union negotiated a cease-fire on October 22. Even though the Israelis achieved an amazing turn-around after early losses, during this war they did suffer high casualties. The Arabs felt that they had fought with honor, unlike in the rout of 1967, and glimpsed an exhilarating new reality—the Israelis might not be invincible after all.

U.S. President Jimmy Carter brought Menachem Begin, now the prime minister of Israel, and Egyptian president Anwar Sadat together at Camp David in September 1978 to sign a historic peace treaty between their nations. Even though Egypt was just one Arab country, many Israelis hoped that peace in the Middle East was finally at hand. But less than four months later, followers of a radical Shiite cleric, the Ayatollah Khomeini, launched a revolution to overthrow Mohammad Reza Pahlavi, the shah of Iran and the only leader in the region to maintain amicable relations with Israel. By December 1979 Islamic revolutionaries had succeeded in installing the Ayatollah Khomeini as the supreme leader of Iran. His rise to power marked the first of many political triumphs for fundamentalist Islam, an ideology that called for Israel's destruction and tapped into the religious identity of at least some of the world's 1.2 billion Muslims.

Two years later, Sunni fundamentalists belonging to an Egyptian underground organization, the Muslim Brotherhood, assassinated President Sadat in revenge for concluding the Camp David peace agreement with Israel. Whereas in 1948 the Jewish state had only to contend with its Arab neighbors, by 1979 its enemy list had grown exponentially and encompassed much of the Muslim world.

Lebanon

When Israeli intelligence learned that the Palestine Liberation Organization (PLO), an organization sworn to destroy the Jewish state, had placed missiles on the Lebanon side of the border it shared with Israel, the IDF launched an invasion in the summer of 1982. The PLO was forced to withdraw from southern Lebanon after the signing of a cease-fire agreement in August 1982. Israeli troops occupied the territory in hopes that it would serve as a buffer against future Arab attacks. But what arose in place of the PLO was the even more militant Shiite movement called Hezbollah—"Party of God"—which Israel, the United States, and other Western countries designated a terrorist organization. Its leaders had been inspired by the Islamic revolution in Iran and trained by the Ayatollah Khomeini's Revolutionary Guards.

Between September 16, 1982, and September 18, 1982, the IDF allowed the Lebanese Christian militia known as the Phalange to enter two refugee camps, and the Phalangists proceeded to massacre 3,500 Palestinians, mostly women and children. The UN condemned the killings and declared them to be an act of genocide, and Europe saw an immediate rise in the number of anti-Semitic incidents. The Israeli government set up the Kahan Commission to investigate the tragedy. The commission's report called for the dismissal of Ariel Sharon as minister of defense, stating:

> It is our view that responsibility is to be imputed to the minister of defense for having disregarded the prospect of acts of vengeance and bloodshed by the Phalangists against the population of the refugee camps and for having failed to take this danger into account when he decided to have the Phalangists enter the camps. In addition, responsibility is to be imputed to the minister of defense for not ordering appropriate measures for preventing or reducing the chances of a massacre as a condition for the Phalangists' entry into the camps.

In 2008 Israeli filmmaker, Ari Folman, came out with the critically acclaimed *Waltz with Bashir*. This animated quasi-documentary film presented his fractured memories as a nineteen-year-old IDF soldier who had been on duty guarding the Palestinian refugee camps in 1982. He had suppressed memories of the three-day period in the Palestinians were slaughtered by soldiers from the Phalange, who were allies of Israel. In interviews, Folman expressed a hope that young Israelis who saw the movie would react by refusing to serve in the IDF.

Between 1982 and 2000, Hezbollah waged a guerrilla campaign against the Israeli forces occupying Southern Lebanon. It consisted of a guerrilla campaign that utilized suicide bombing attacks on IDF forces and Israeli civilians and kidnappings. Israel withdrew from southern

Lebanon in the summer of 2000, a move interpreted in the Arab world as a victory for Hezbollah.

However, on July 12, 2006, Hezbollah soldiers launched an antitank missile attack against an IDF patrol while firing rockets at Israeli border towns as a diversionary tactic. Two Israeli soldiers were captured. The Jewish state responded to this provocation by invading Lebanon. Amnesty International assessed the damage caused by the ensuing war in a report issued in August 2006:

> During more than four weeks of ground and aerial bombardment of Lebanon by the Israeli armed forces, the country's infrastructure suffered destruction on a catastrophic scale. Israeli forces pounded buildings into the ground, reducing entire neighborhoods to rubble and turning villages and towns into ghost towns. . . . Entire families were killed in air strikes on their homes or in their vehicles while fleeing the aerial assaults on their villages. . . . In addition to the human toll—an estimated 1,183 fatalities, about one third of whom have been children, 4,054 people injured and 970,000 Lebanese people displaced—the civilian infrastructure was severely damaged.[16]

Hezbollah declared victory merely on account of having survived the Israel bombardment of Lebanon, bringing yet another unanticipated setback for the Jewish state. The myth of Israel's military invincibility crumbled under the weight of incoming Katyusha rockets. Hezbollah, supplied by Syria and Iran, could not be dislodged from its strongholds. The international community castigated Israel for its bombing of civilian targets, further isolating the Jewish state from other members of the global community. Even opinion polls in the United States, Israel's staunchest ally, showed growing dissatisfaction with its pursuit of the war in Lebanon.

The Intifadas
In December 1987 spontaneous Palestinian uprisings erupted in Gaza and the West Bank in response to difficult living conditions in the Occupied Territories. John Mearsheimer, a political science professor at the University of Chicago, and Stephen Walt, an international relations professor at Harvard University, asserted:

During the first intifada, the [Israel Defense Forces] distributed trun-cheons to its troops and encouraged them to break the bones of Pales-tinian protesters. The Swedish branch of Save the Children estimated that 23,600 to 29,000 children required medical treatment for their beating injuries in the first two years of the intifada. Nearly a third of them were aged ten or under.[17]

By the time hostilities subsided six years after the beginning of the First Intifada, 1,282 Palestinians and 160 Israelis were dead.[18] The Bank of Israel estimated that the uprising had cost the country more than $650 million in lost exports.[19]

The Second Intifada began in September 2000, when a visit by Israeli prime minister Ariel Sharon to East Jerusalem prompted false rumors that the Jews intended to blow up sacred Muslim holy sites. A truce was signed between Israel and Hamas in June 2008. But by then, Palestinian deaths totaled 5,322, and 1,057 Israelis had been killed. Included in those figures were even more tragic numbers. There were 119 Israeli and 982 Palestin-ian children killed during this conflict.[20] In January 2009, as Israeli tanks rolled into Gaza, Palestinian leaders were warning of a third intifada.

Hamas

Two members of the Palestinian branch of the radical Muslim Brother-hood, Muhammad Taha and Sheikh Ahmed Yassin, used the highly charged political climate of the First Intifada in order to organize a new political party—Hamas. Working underground for nearly two decades, establish-ing hospitals, schools, and other social services in the Palestinian areas, it only rose to international notice in its dramatic 2006 electoral victory.

Hamas, which was in some ways a Sunni version of the Shiite Hezbollah, rose to power primarily in Gaza. Its political and paramilitary wings casti-gated the more secularized PLO for corruption and being insufficiently ag-gressive. Even though Hamas called for jihad against Israel, Professor Uri Avnery asserted that the Jewish state was largely responsible for the party's exist-ence. He declared:

For years, the occupation authorities favored the Islamic movement in the occupied territories. All other political activities were rigorously suppressed, but their activities in the mosques were permitted. The calculation was simple and naive: at the time, the PLO was considered the main enemy, Yasser Arafat was the current Satan. The Islamic movement was preaching against the PLO and Arafat, and was therefore viewed as an ally.[21]

The U.S. State Department identified the sources of Hamas's funding as Saudi Arabia, Iran, Palestinian expatriates, and private benefactors in other Arab countries.[22]

In the 2006 Gaza elections, Hamas stunned Israeli and U.S. observers by winning the majority of seats in Parliament and local offices. The Jewish state now faced a new dilemma. What could it do when the democratically elected party among the Palestinians also happened to be an internationally recognized terrorist organization?

Gaza War

Israel closed all border crossings with Gaza, asphyxiating the occupied territory's already weak economy. On December 23, 2008, leaders of Hamas declared the end of a six-month cease-fire with Israel. The next day they issued a statement declaring their willingness to renew the cease-fire agreement if Israel lifted its economic strangulation of Gaza. In the meantime, Hamas continued to lob primitive Kassam rockets at southern Israel. Four days later, Israel launched a massive aerial attack on the Gaza Strip. Some observers believed that the timing of the Israeli attacks corresponded with both a heated Israeli election campaign and the fact that President George W. Bush would be leaving the presidency in three weeks' time and the president-elect, Barack Obama, might not show the same level of loyalty toward Israel. A December 27, 2008, article in the *New York Times* summed up the situation leading to the complete breakdown of the cease-fire and the dramatic increase in hostilities:

> Opening the routes to commerce was Hamas's main goal in its cease-fire with Israel, just as ending the rocket fire was Israel's central aim. But while rocket fire did go down drastically in the fall to 15 to 20 a month from hundreds a month, Israel said it would not permit trade to begin again because the rocket fire had not completely stopped and because Hamas continued to smuggle weapons from Egypt through desert tunnels. Hamas said this was a violation of the agreement, a sign

of Israel's real intentions and cause for further rocket fire. On Wednesday [12/24/08], some 70 rockets hit Israel over 24 hours, in a distinct increase in intensity.[23]

Israel's strategic concept may have been to pressure the population of Gaza to overthrow Hamas in order to install Mahmoud Abbas as leader of the Palestinian Authority on the West Bank. But a war that has cost more than 1,000 Palestinian lives, half of which were women and children, weakened rather than strengthened the moderate Arab states, which preached coexistence with Israel. The Israelis also miscalculated the degree to which the Hamas Party, thus including its military wing, was interwoven with the fabric of Gazan society. In the aftermath of the war, human rights groups even charged top Israeli officials with war crimes, making international travel difficult for some.

4

The Demographic Minefield

However well the Israelis trained to confront their enemies, there was one war they could not win—the demographic one. Testifying before the Knesset Foreign Affairs and Defense Committee, Professor Arnon Sofer of Haifa University declared that unless the population problems relating to the higher birthrate among Arabs compared to Jews are solved "our country is finished in 17 years, and there will be a collapse."[1] California businessman Ron Unz commented in a 2002 letter to *Commentary Magazine*: ". . . I expect [Israel's] trajectory to follow that of the temporary Crusader kingdoms, surviving for seventy or eighty years after its establishment in 1948 and then collapsing under continual Muslim pressure and flagging ideological commitment."[2]

In 2008 the state's Jewish population numbered approximately 5.5 million. The Palestinian residents within Israel proper was calculated at just over a million. The number of Palestinians living on the West Bank and Gaza was approximately 3.5 million. They also had high birthrates (6 children per mother), compared to the Jewish population of Israel (2.6 children per mother). Adding Palestinians in the diaspora, including temporary workers in other Middle Eastern countries, brought that number to nearly 9 million. There were 310 million non-Palestinian Arabs in the region, almost all of whom were sympathetic to the Palestinian cause. The number of Muslims of non-Arab ethnicity, including Iranians, Afghanis, Pakistanis, and Indonesians, who also evinced anti-Israeli attitudes hovered around 1.2 billion people—20 percent of the world's population.

Land without a People
Confusion surrounds what the early twentieth-century Zionists may or may not have believed in regard to the demographics of the Middle East when they set their sights on creating a Jewish state. But the Zionist slogan, "Israel is a land without a people for a people without land," may turn out to be a miscalculation so breathtaking in its naiveté that it could ultimately cost Israel its hard-fought Jewish statehood.

Debate surrounds who first coined the phrase, although Alexander Keith, a minister in the Church of Scotland, published *The Land of Israel According to the Covenant with Abraham, with Isaac, and with Jacob* in 1844. The book stated that the Jews are "a people without a country; even as their own land, as subsequently to be shown, is in a great measure a country without a people."[3]

An even bigger argument surrounds whether the saying "A land without a people for a people without a land" became an official slogan of the Zionists or was just a catchy phrase that caught on. In 2008 historian Diana Muir wrote an article in the *Middle Eastern Quarterly* entitled "A Land without a People for a People without a Land." She argued that the phrase was used by late-nineteenth century Christians in the United States and Britain who advocated Jewish, rather than Zionist, settlement in Palestine.

However, a book written by Professor Norman Dwight Harris in 1926 entitled *Europe and the East* would suggest otherwise. In it he chastised "the over-zealous efforts of the Zionist Executive Commission," declaring: "Their very slogan, 'The land without a people for the people without a land,' was an insult to the Arabs of the country."[4]

Harris then noted:

> The reaction against this short-sighted, selfish policy was immediate. A determined opposition to the Zionist movement arose throughout the country, which increased rapidly till it embraced nine tenths of the population, including many orthodox Jews. Riots occurred in Jerusa-

lem and other cities. And there ensued a rapid development of Arab national consciousness—totally unexpected by the British authorities.[5]

Journalist Steven Poole has also attempted to clarify use of this slogan by asserting:

> The specific claim was not the blatantly false one that the territory was unpopulated, nor that those living there were not human, but that they did not constitute "a people": in other words, it was argued that they had no conception of nationhood in the modern western sense.[6]

Whether or not the Palestinians were seen as a nation or just a conglomeration of amorphous Arab villagers, early Zionists attempted to win the demographic war by resettling as many Jews as possible to their ancestral homeland. David Ben-Gurion stated in 1933: "In the course of four to five years we must bring in a quarter of a million Jews and the Arab question will be solved."[7] But four years later, Ze'ev Jabotinsky, always the realist, declared that the problems they faced would not be as easily surmounted merely through more favorable Jewish demographics as the early Zionists had believed. He asserted:

> There is no point talking about the possibility that the Arabs in Eretz Israel would consent to the Zionist plan while we are a minority here. . . . Every indigenous people, regardless of whether it is primitive or advanced, views its country as a national home and aspires to be and remain its sole and eternal landlord; it does not voluntarily agree to accommodate, not only new landlords, but even new partners or new participants. And our most misleading argument would be to rely on the fact that our agricultural settlements bring them economical advantages. Though this is an undisputed truth, there is no nation in the world that sold its national aspirations for bread and butter.[8]

In large part, Jabotinsky was deriding notions promulgated by Theodor Herzl. Herzl believed that European Jews would bring their technical expertise to the Middle East, raising standards of living for all and winning the everlasting gratitude of the "primitive and backward" Arabs.[9] In 1902 Herzl published a utopian novel called *Altneuland* (Old New Land). At one point in the story the Muslim-Arab protagonist Rashid Bey declares: "The Jews have enriched us. Why should we be angry with them? They dwell among us like brothers. Why should we not love them?"[10]

The Debate over Arab Expulsion

Zionist writings during the World War II period reflect an intense debate over whether Arabs should be transferred or expelled from Palestine in order to make way for the creation of a Jewish state. No master plan has ever been found that suggested explicit orders were drawn up by Jewish leaders to expel Palestinians from their homes. However, Israeli government and political party documents declassified in the 1980s did reveal a vigorous exchange of ideas on the subject. On October 5, 1937, Ben-Gurion wrote to his son, Amos:

> We do not wish and do not need to expel Arabs and take their place. All our aspiration is built on the assumption—proven throughout all our activity—that there is enough room for ourselves and the Arabs in Palestine. But if the Arabs did not accept that assumption, and if we have to use force—not to dispossess the Arabs of the Negev and Transjordan, but to guarantee our own right to settle in those places— then we have force at our disposal.[11]

The Law of Return

With the establishment of the state of Israel in 1948, *Aliya*—"the Law of Return"—became the centerpiece of the nation's Jewish statehood. It allowed Jews anywhere in the world to obtain Israeli citizenship. With immigration restrictions now lifted, Jews from Eastern Europe, who confronted renewed persecution, streamed into Israel. Between 1949 and 1950, 49,000 Yemeni Jews were airlifted to Israel. One hundred and fourteen thousand Iraqi Jews relocated to Israel in 1951. After the Iranian Revolution of 1979, 30,000 Iranian Jews arrived in Israel. In the 1980s Ethiopian Jews were airlifted to Israel and now number more than 100,000. The collapse of the Soviet Union in the early 1990s allowed for the lifting of immigration restrictions and the resettlement of a million Russian Jews in Israel. Because they were allowed to bring with them Russian Orthodox Christian family members and relatives, nearly a half of all Russian immigrants were not Jewish. The Israeli government accepted claims of membership in large Russian extended families for which only one member need claim (but not prove) Jewish ancestry.

The Benei Menashe Jews from India, claiming to be a lost tribe of Israel, also began moving to Israel in the 1990s. With the collapse of the Argentine economy in 1999, more than 10,000 Jews from that country made their way to Israel in order to make a fresh start. Anti-Semitic violence rose in France in the early 2000s, prompting more than 11,000 French Jews to "make aliyah," or to voluntarily immigrate to Eretz Israel. However, these numbers were not adding up in the way the framers of the Jewish state had originally intended. Even though 110,000 North American Jews had relocated to Israel, the majority of American and European Jews were not emigrating.

The No-Return Policy
In comparison to European Jews and their non-Jewish relatives, Ethiopians and East Indian tribes asserting rights to Israeli citizenship, Palestinians were given a thirty-three-year waiting period for the processing of their citizenship applications. This was even the case for those whose immediate families had been forcibly removed to make way for the Jewish state and possessed documents to prove land ownership in particular Israeli villages. The fact that Israel adopted a "no return policy" for Arab refugees in contradistinction to the law of return for Jews in the diaspora solved the problem of how to set up a Jewish state in an Arab world. However, it also transformed the dynamics of what started out as an internal conflict between Palestinians and Jews into a permanent state of war with the Jews on one side and the Arab and Muslim world on the other.

Not surprising, many Israelis have come to fear the community of Palestinian citizens within Israel proper, as a fifth column of potential traitors and saboteurs. Many Palestinian extended families have members on both sides of the border. In October 2000, during the Second Intifada, Israeli security forces killed thirteen Arab-Israeli protestors who were demonstrating in solidarity with the Palestinians in the Occupied Territories. Professor Benny Morris warned:

> The Israeli Arabs are a time bomb. Their slide into complete Palestinization has made them an emissary of the enemy that is among us. They are a potential fifth column. In both demographic

and security terms they are liable to undermine the state. So that if Israel again finds itself in a situation of existential threat, as in 1948, it may be forced to act as it did then. If we are attacked by Egypt (after an Islamist revolution in Cairo) and by Syria, and chemical and biological missiles slam into our cities, and at the same time Israeli Palestinians attack us from behind, I can see an expulsion situation. It could happen. If the threat to Israel is existential, expulsion will be justified.[12]

The Occupied Territories

Israeli fears of an Arab majority in its democratically ruled nation explained the receptivity of Jewish political leaders to peace initiatives calling for the establishment of a separate Palestinian state, even though their entreaties have been undermined by continuing Jewish settlements on the West Bank. Jeffrey Goldberg, writing in the *Atlantic Monthly*, observed:

> The demographic trend has raised fears that Israel will become a state like pre-Mandela South Africa, in which the minority ruled the majority. But if the Arabs of the West Bank and Gaza were given the vote, then Israel, a country, whose fundamental purpose has been to serve as a refuge for persecuted Jews, and to allow those Jews to have the novel experience of being part of a majority, would disappear, to be replaced by an Arab-dominated "one-state" state. Yet Israel has not found a way to escape the West Bank.[13]

When Israel was founded in 1948, Zionist leaders assumed that these refugees would become absorbed into the surrounding Arab states eventually. The Zionists underestimated the emergence of Palestinian nationalism, just as the world may have misunderstood their Jewish nationalism. Israeli leaders also believed that most of the world's Jewry would immigrate to Israel. The fact that this did not happen embittered some Israelis toward American Jews and other communities in the diaspora.

The Democracy Dilemma

How was Israel to maintain its Jewish majority if Arab citizens of the country reached a majority? Demographers now say this will happen in the next forty years. Whereas Middle Eastern Jews, who now constitute a

majority of the Israeli population, once had high birth rates, such is no longer the case. Recent statistics show that the Mizrahim or Sephardim birthrates are nearly comparable to that of the Ashkenazim Jews. Ultra-religious Jews, conversely, believe that having large families is a requirement of their religion, and they maintain a birthrate comparable to that of Palestinians. But this race to birth as many orthodox Jewish children as possible strains the secular nature of the Jewish state.[14] It is also questionable whether basing this land-scarce nation's future on a fertility race between orthodox Jews and Arabs will be of long-range social benefit.

Had Israel perceived itself as a totalitarian state, things might have worked out as planned. But its sense of itself as a liberal democracy and a Jewish state meant that the Jewish majority would have to be protected. And that was not going to be easy. Israeli politics have been beset with political schemes aimed at securing the Jewish majority while maintaining the semblance of democratic governance. The right wing within Israeli politics believed that the focus needed to be on doing whatever was necessary not to endanger the Jewishness of the state, even if that meant suspending some of the more liberal democratic ideals. The Left, meanwhile, worried that political preoccupations with maintaining the Jewish orientation of the state would undermine its fundamental democratic-ness.

5

Apocalypse Fever

Katyusha rocket barrages fired from enemy territory and demographics are not the only nightmares disturbing the sleep of Israeli Jews. The specter of a nuclear-armed Iran is an issue that touches on their deepest fears of being wiped off the face of the planet. Israeli prime minister Benjamin Netanyahu, announced to a pro-Israel crowd in Los Angeles, "It's 1938 and Iran is Germany and Iran is racing to arm itself with atomic bombs." But it is Kenneth Timmerman, an American journalist, who has been leading the charge. His book, *Countdown to Crisis: The Coming Nuclear Showdown with Iran,* asserts that the U.S. intelligence community covered up Iranian involvement in the September 11, 2001, attack on the World Trade Center and Pentagon.[1] He has been accused of stoking conflict with Iran (a charge that his supporters deny) by misrepresenting the threat of an Iranian nuclear weapons program, as well as denouncing the National Intelligence Estimates, which summarize the conclusions of the U.S. intelligence community. Those reports state that the Iranians had ended a project to design nuclear warheads years ago, although they had increased their efforts on the more important parts of their program for building nuclear weapons.[2] Even though intelligence reports dispute his claims, Timmerman's book has remained on Israeli bestseller lists since its publication in 2005. Dr. Amy Rosenbluh, a research microbiologist and mayor of a West Bank settlement, has also warned:

> The Iranian nuclear threat, as the proliferation of nuclear weapons anywhere in the Moslem world, is a clear and undeniable clarion call to the entire Western world. It is unthinkable, a mere seventy years after Hitler made good on his threatened attempt to world domination, that a similar challenge by yet another fanatic go unheeded.[3]

Robert Baer, a former CIA case officer, wrote in a September 27, 2008, *New York Daily News* column that President Bush had earlier in the year "nixed an Israeli plan to attack Iran's nuclear facilities." [4] Bush feared Iranian retaliation against U.S. troops in Iraq and Afghanistan, as well as the possibility of Iran closing down shipping that passes through the Persian Gulf, the Strait of Hormuz, and the Gulf of Oman. In such a case "Americans could suddenly be looking at the prospect of $10–$12 for a gallon of gas." [5] But Baer went on to warn, "None of this changes the fact that Israel—on its own, without U.S. complicity—is moving closer to a decision to attack Iran, almost by the day." [6]

"Israel Could Survive a Nuclear War" was the headline of a *Jerusalem Post* article on December 24, 2007. The reporter, Elie Leshem, quoted a report prepared by the Center for Strategic and International Studies (CSIS) in Washington, D.C., in which the casualty breakdown was 16 million–20 million Iranians dead compared to 200,000–800,000 Israelis.[7]

Whether other nations believe the Middle East is poised on the brink of nuclear war, many Israelis do, and they are armed to the teeth. In a 2008 press conference, former president Jimmy Carter revealed that Israel has "one hundred and fifty or more nuclear weapons." [8] In 2007 alone the United States gave Israel "a load of 500 ton nuclear tipped bunker busting bombs." There has been much discussion in Israel of making preemptive strikes on Iran in the same vein as the 1981 Israeli bombing of Iraq's nuclear facilities. Professor Benny Morris explored some of the difficulties involved in such an operation. He asserted:

> Taking their cue from the successful Israel Air Force's destruction in 1981 of Iraq's Osiraq nuclear reactor, the Iranians duplicated and

dispersed their facilities and buried them deep underground (and the Iranian targets are about twice as far from Israel as was Baghdad).[9]

The Oxford Research Group also released a report in February 2006 suggesting that the consequences of such an attack would be far more catastrophic than the Iraq bombing. The report declared:

> Iran . . . would see any Israeli action as being done in close collaboration with the United States, and would respond against U.S. and Gulf oil interests in much the same way as if the attacks had been conducted by the United States itself. This would, in turn, bring U.S. forces into the confrontation as the United States reacted to such moves. Any such escalation of the war would be of value to Israel as it would tend to weaken the wider military capabilities of Iran. Thus, Israeli action would be intended to severely damage Iranian nuclear potential while being likely to bring the United States into the conflict. Iran's more direct reaction to Israeli military action might be to put substantial emphasis on encouraging Hezbollah to act against Israel, possibly through missile attacks into Northern Israel.[10]

However, the London *Telegraph* reported in February 2009 that Israel's Mossad espionage agency may have even embarked on a program of assassinating Iranian nuclear physicists rather than risk the global political fallout from an attack on that country's nuclear facilities. The *Telegraph* reported that "[Israel] is using hitmen, sabotage, front companies and double agents to disrupt [Iran's] illicit weapons."[11] It also quoted Reva Bhalla, a senior analyst at the American private intelligence company, Stratfor, that "with co-operation from the United States, Israeli covert operations have focused both on eliminating key human assets involved in the nuclear programme and in sabotaging the Iranian nuclear supply chain."[12]

Not surprisingly, many Israelis contemplating the prospect of yet another war find themselves depressed and exhausted, struggling with a growing sense of futility and the recklessness it breeds. Israeli novelist David Grossman remarked in a 2008 interview:

> If you see the tendencies of fanaticism, the way in which at every crossroads both sides almost always choose the more violent approach,

if you see the fact that other religions, parts of the West, never really accept the idea of Israel. . . . It means something deep about us (and even more about everyone else), about Judaism and the state that we are still in, after 60 years of sovereignty—we have not accomplished statehood, the realization that this is a legitimate state. . . . confidence in our own existence. We also don't really believe in our own existence. We have the formal symptoms of a normal state, but we still do not believe we are a state.[13]

A Second Holocaust?

In 1993 author Philip Roth published *Operation Shylock: A Confession*, a novel that coined the term "second Holocaust." In an exchange with the novel's narrator, a character called the Diasporist opined:

> The meanings of the Holocaust," he replied gravely, "are for us to determine, but one thing is sure—its meaning will be no less tragic than it is now if there is a second Holocaust and the offspring of the European Jews who evacuated Europe for a seemingly safer haven should meet collective annihilation in the Middle East . . . but a second Holocaust could happen here all too easily, and, if the conflict between Arab and Jew escalates much longer, it will—it must. The destruction of Israel in a nuclear exchange is a possibility much less far-fetched today than was the Holocaust itself fifty years ago.[14]

A decade and a half after Roth's book came out, the Anti-Defamation League conducted a poll of Jewish attitudes toward the future. It revealed that one-third of Jewish Israeli youth considered a second Holocaust to be a real possibility.[15] Professor Benny Morris, in an article entitled "The Second Holocaust Is Looming," painted a spine-chilling scenario of Israel's future:

> One bright morning, in five or ten years' time, perhaps during a regional crisis, perhaps out of the blue, a day or a year or five years after Iran's acquisition of the Bomb, the mullahs in Qom will covoke in secret session, under a portrait of the steely-eyed Ayatollah Khomeini, and give President Ahmedinejad, by then in his second or third term, the go ahead. The orders will go out and the Shihab III and IV missiles will

take off for Tel Aviv, Beersheba, Haifa, and Jerusalem, and probably some military sites, including Israel's half dozen air and (reported) nuclear missile bases. . . . With a country the size and shape of Israel (an elongated 8,000 square miles), probably four or five hits will suffice: No more Israel. A million or more Israelis, in the greater Tel Aviv, Haifa and Jerusalem areas, will die immediately. Millions will be seriously irradiated.

Professor Morris posited that while some of the dead would be Arabs living in Israel proper or the Occupied Territories, the Iranians could not care less. He said, "The Iranians don't especially like Arabs, especially Sunni Arabs, with whom they have intermittently warred for centuries."[16]

Armageddon

The more traumatized Jewish Israelis become in sensing their sovereignty slipping away, the more casual talk of using its nuclear arsenal becomes, preemptively in a we'd-rather-go-down-fighting spirit. But there is an even more ominous threat on the horizon—religious zealots. Christian, Muslim, and Jewish ones are converging on this region, seeming almost to hanker for apocalyptic upheaval.

Christian evangelicals like the deceased Jerry Falwell and Pat Robertson believe that the establishment of the modern nation of Israel has been a vital step in fulfilling biblical prophecy. Grace Halsell lamented in her book *Prophecy and Politics: Militant Evangelists on the Road to Nuclear War*, "One disappointed Christian tourist found that for every hour spent at Christian sites and hearing about Jesus, thirty were spent extolling the political and military achievements of Israel."[17]

The theological concept of eschatology refers to religious beliefs regarding the end of the world. Popular Christian interpretations of the Bible regarding the apocalypse come from a theology known as premillennial dispensationalism, whose origins can be traced back to nineteenth-century England. Professor Donald E. Wagner explained:

The preaching and writings of a renegade Irish clergyman, John Nelson Darby, and a Scottish evangelist, Edward Irving, emphasized the literal and future fulfillment of such teachings as the Rapture, the rise of the

Antichrist, the Battle of Armageddon, and the central role that a re-
vived state of Israel would play during the end days.[18]

Reverend Darby brought these teachings to the United States and
influenced popular American evangelists, including Cyrus I. Scofield.
According to Wagner:

> Scofield applied Darby's eschatology to his version of the scriptures
> and provided an outline of premillennial dispensationalist notations of
> the text. The Scofield Bible (1909) gave dispensationalist teachings
> much of their prominence and popularity. It became the Bible version
> used by most evangelical and fundamentalist Christians for the next
> 60 years.[19]

When Hal Lindsey and Carole C. Carlson's bestseller *The Late, Great
Planet Earth* came out in 1970, American audiences were exposed to end
time scenarios involving climactic events leading to the rise of the anti-
Christ and the "Rapture," in which Christians dead and alive will be taken
up to Heaven, followed by the Second Coming of Jesus Christ. Lindsey
and Carlson's book prophesized that end time events would begin to un-
fold one generation after the 1948 rebirth of Israel.[20] Ten years later they
came out with *The 1980s: Countdown to Armageddon*, sparking a surge
in the market for doomsday books relating to Christian eschatology. In
1995 Tim LaHaye and Jerry B. Jenkins published *Left Behind: A Novel
of the Earth's Last Days*. This was the first book in a series of sixteen
bestselling novels that told the story of events surrounding the end times,
which included the Rapture, the emergence of the anti-Christ, and the
continuing struggle of a group of survivors who fought against the de-
scending chaos.

The publication of Michael Drosnin's bestseller *The Bible Code* in 1998
and its sequel, *Bible Code II: The Countdown*, have added to the hysteria of
religious fundamentalists. Thus far his predictions have bombed. They included a smallpox bacterium attack on Israel in 2005 that would kill 14,700
and major meteor strikes and/or nuclear war in the years 2000 or 2006.
But what they did do was move some Christian and Jewish fundamentalists into a convergence of end time theologies around a date, ironically,
first articulated by the Mayans, a pagan civilization on the other side of the

globe. According to the prophesiers, the end of the world as we know it is supposed to occur in 2012, thus merging the biblical end of days with the specific December 21 date circulating in New Age and Latin American circles.

The Temple Mount

Professors Norton Mezvinsky and Israel Shahak, authors of *Jewish Fundamentalism in Israel*, have written that

> Some varieties of Jewish fundamentalism are clearly more dangerous than others. Jewish fundamentalism is not only capable of influencing conventional Israeli policies but could also substantially affect Israeli nuclear policies.[21]

Traditional Judaism has long held that the Messiah would come as an act of redemption for Israel, forgiving the sins of his people and fulfilling his eternal promises to them. This "redemption" could not be hastened by human actions. However, in the 1920s the writings of Rabbi Abraham Isaac Kook (1865–1935) reinterpreted the scriptures. He proclaimed that Zionists, even those who professed atheism, were the unwitting agents of God, ushering in the messianic age. His son, Rabbi Zvi Yehuda Kook (1891–1982), preached that the very presence of Jews on the land redeemed it from unholiness, thus providing a theological basis for the Jewish settlement movement.

However, a growing number of Jewish groups intent on triggering the apocalypse clock also believe that certain conditions must be met in order for the end times prophecy to be fulfilled. First and foremost is the construction of the Third Temple on the Temple Mount where Solomon's Temple once stood, the holiest site in Judaism. The Babylonians razed it to the ground in 586 BCE. The Jewish community built the Second Temple seventy years later on the same site. The Romans destroyed it in 70 CE, dispersing the Jews to lands outside of Palestine. The messianic yearning for the construction of a Third Temple is articulated in the thrice-daily prayer service of Orthodox Jews.[22]

Christian "dispensationalists" also believe that Jews must rebuild the temple so that Jesus Christ can return and sit on a throne prepared specially for him there. But there is a glitch. The Temple Mount is also one of the most revered places in Islam. The Dome of the Rock, a magnificent structure built in 691 CE, is the oldest mosque still in existence.

In 1969 an Australian mental patient set fire to the Dome of the Rock, which sparked rioting among Muslims of Jerusalem. Rabbi Meir Kahane, founder of the militant Jewish Defense League, was jailed for several months in 1980 for plotting to destroy the Dome of the Rock. Rabbi Kahane established the Kach Party in 1973, whose platform called for the annexation of all conquered territories and the forcible expulsion of the Palestinians.

In 1983 Rabbi Kahane published *Forty Years*, a book that gave the Jews a specified period of time to please God through creation of a theocracy, which included the cleansing of the Temple Mount. "If 'the Jew' passed the test, redemption would come peacefully. If not, it would be preceded by a 'needless holocaust,' more horrible than anything we have yet endured."[23]

The next year, the Israeli police uncovered a plot to blow up the Al-Aqsa mosque and the Dome of the Rock. Behind the plot were Ben Shoshan and Yehuda Etzion, both members of the Jewish Gush Emunim (the Bloc of Fidelity) an underground Israeli political movement founded in 1974 by students of Rabbi Zvi Yehuda Kook. The two men believed that destroying those Muslim holy sites would cause a spiritual awakening in Israel. They also hoped the Third Temple of Jerusalem would be built on the location of the destroyed mosques. However, before the plot could be carried out, Israeli police (Shin Bet agents) arrested Etzion and other conspirators who had set powerful bombs on the undercarriage of five Arab buses, set to detonate during the apex of rush hour.[24] While serving a seven-year prison term, Etzion mobilized an even larger following for this cause through publication of his book, *Temple Mount*. He argued that God considered the Muslim Dome of the Rock and Al-Aqsa Mosque pollutants and that "the expurgation of the Temple Mount will prepare the hearts for the understanding and further advancing of our full redemption."[25] By 1989 Etzion had rejoined civilian life, declaring that his mistake had merely been a tactical one in acting too quickly. He constructed a new movement called Hai Vekayam, which means everlasting. Israeli journalist Gershom Gorenberg, author of *The End of Days: Fundamentalism and the Struggle for the Temple Mount*, has warned: "The Temple Mount beckons seductively to believers eager to restart redemption." Gorenberg interviewed Etzion, who explained his movement's goals, declaring: "A group will arise that will know how to translate the desire into action."[26]

In fact, more than 100 attempts have been made since 1967 to destroy the Dome of the Rock or the adjacent Al-Aqsa Mosque by various factions of the Jewish underground. A group calling itself the Temple Mount and Eretz Yisrael Faithful Movement is made up of Orthodox Jews who have pressured the Israeli government, thus far in vain, to relocate Al-Aqsa Mosque and the Dome of the Rock to the Muslim holy city of Mecca in Saudi Arabia. The Second Intifada—also known as the Al-Aqsa Intifida—erupted on September 29, 2000, one day after Prime Minister Ariel Sharon, surrounded by armed guards, visited Al-Aqsa Mosque and the Temple Mount. Rumors spread through the Palestinian quarters of Jerusalem that the Israelis were intending to destroy the mosque to make way for construction of their Third Temple. A spontaneous uprising ensued in which the death toll between 2000 and 2008 has been 5,322 Palestinians and 1,057 Israelis.[27]

The Four-Legged Bomb

A judge who tried the 1984 case of the Jewish settler underground's plot to blow up the Dome of the Rock declared that had the plan succeeded, it would have "exposed the State of Israel and the entire Jewish people to a new Holocaust." Leaders of the extremist group explained that they were impeded from entering the Temple Mount because of an inability to purify themselves spiritually, which would have required the "ash of a red heifer."[28] Abrahamic tradition makes reference to a sacrificial red heifer, known in Hebrew as *parah adumah,* whose ashes were used for purposes of ritual purification for people who came into contact with a corpse. According to the nineteenth chapter of Numbers in the Hebrew Bible, verse e: "Speak unto the children, that they bring thee a red heifer without spot, wherein is no blemish, and upon which never came yoke."

The state of ritual purity obtained through the ashes of a red heifer is a necessary prerequisite for participating in any Third Temple service. However, "the last certified ashes ran out shortly after the Second Temple was destroyed by the Romans in 70 A.D., and since then, the absence of new ashes has been one of the obstacles to reconstructing the Temple," declared a report in the *New York Times* on June 14, 1997.[29] The article went on to explain the spotlight being given to Melody, a red calf born at an Israeli agricultural college near Haifa in August 1996, whose appearance signaled to some religious observers that the end of the world was drawing near. However, Melody disappointed the rabbis who had declared her birth a miracle when she sprouted a clump of white hairs at the tip of her tail at the age of one and a half years. Six years before, a Southern Baptist cattleman from Mississippi named Reverend Clyde Lott traveled to Jerusalem and met with Rabbi Yisrael Ariel of the Temple Institute to initiate a Red Angus breeding program in Israel that would ensure the birth of a red heifer on Jewish soil.[30] Lott created a nonprofit organization called the Canaan Land Restoration of Israel, Inc., to raise funds for transporting 200 pregnant cows to Israel. However, Lott had a falling out with the rabbis when they learned of his intention to convert Jews to Christianity.[31]

David Landau, a columnist for the Israeli daily *Haaretz*, called the search for the red heifer "s four-legged bomb." Landau warned that the security services should recognize this threat as "potentially more dangerous than any terrorist."

The Temple Institute

Rabbi Ariel founded the Machon HaMikdash (Temple Institute) in 1987 to prepare for construction of the Third Temple on the site of Islam's sacred Dome of the Rock Mosque. The institute has commissioned the sewing of ritual garments and the development of blueprints for the temple's construction. In December 2007 the Temple Institute announced completion of the *tzitz*, or the High Priest's headplate. Rabbi Chaim Richman, the Temple Institute's international director, also announced that

> we have begun work on 120 sets of garments for "regular" priests, not the High Priest. This involves special thread from India. In addition, we have begun work on architectural blueprints for the Third Temple, including cost projection, modern supplies, electricity, plumbing, computers. . . .[32]

According to the Temple Institute's website, the organization has also completed the making of such ritual objects as the small and large *mizrak*, vessels used to gather blood from animal sacrifices, and the wood and gold lottery box in which "on Yom Kippur, the High Priest reaches into the lottery box and chooses lots. Thus is determined which goat will be used as an offering to G-d, and which will be sent off to *Azazel* [chief of the goat-demons], as an atonement for the sins of the people."[33]

Rabbi Richman is also a member of the Sanhedrin Council, a self-appointed group of 71 prominent rabbis who are attempting to revive the ancient body that served as the highest ruling religious authority in Israel. The original Sanhedrin was dissolved in the late fourth century CE, never having recovered its full power after the 70 CE destruction of the Second Temple. While various Jewish sects have debated the legitimacy of the re-vived Sanhedrin Council, the group has set for itself the task of choosing Israel's first king. It disagrees with the system of democratic governance of the Jewish state. The new Sanhedrin Council also sent a letter to interna-tional heads of state, including Arab leaders, in 2007 "warning that the world is nearing a catastrophe, and that the only way to bring peace on earth is through the rebuilding of the Temple."[34]

The Hour of God's Judgment

Muslim eschatology lays out a number of scenarios associated with the end of the world, differing in accordance with the diverse sects of Islam. Ac-cording to Gorenberg's *The End of Days*:

> In the final days, a false messiah or *al-dajjal*, will appear to conquer the world, leading an army of Jews from the east. At last Jesus will return to defeat the deceiver in a battle near Jerusalem. Afterward he will kill all pigs, break all crosses, and leave Islam as the world's sole faith. In many versions, he shares his role as redeemer with a figure called the *mahdi*. All this is the preface for when the dead rise and every man and woman who ever was faces judgment at the valley of Jehosafat next to Jerusalem's walls.[35]

This concept of the appearance of al-Dajjal (the anti-Christ) who will be defeated by the coming of the Mahdi is prevalent both in Sunni and Shiite Islam. However, eschatology tends to play a larger role in the theol-ogy of Shiism.

The Arab-Israeli conflict has created an opportunity for Islamic fun-damentalists to inject Western anti-Semitic themes into their end time prophecies. Muslim radical Sayyid Qutb is often identified as a principal articulator of this tendency, "using the forged Protocols of the Elders of

Zion and other Western material, accusing Jews of being inherently evil, aggressive, exploiters, manipulators, usurers, and haters of humanity."[36]

Other Muslim fundamentalists, however, caution "against this extreme modern reinterpretation of traditional views, claiming that Muslims and Jews had lived in peaceful relations with each other for many centuries, Islam being tolerant of the *ahl al-kitab* (people of the book) granting them protected status and covenant rights."[37]

Messiah's Donkey

Also feeding the end time narrative has been a controversial book, *Messiah's Donkey*, published in Israel in 1998. According to the author, Seffi Rachlevsky, the religious-national camp in Israel viewed the secular majority in Israel as a donkey. It built the state but must step aside so that the religious community could take power in preparation for the coming of the Messiah. Rachlevsky claimed that the word "donkey" (in Hebrew, *hamor*) came from the word "material" (in Hebrew, *homer*), and referred to the way in which the secular segments of Israeli society were to be the ones building the material reality of the state. By arguing that a conspiratorial ideology was the defining concept of the national religious camp, the author blamed its followers collectively for Yigal Amir's assassination of Israeli Prime Minister Yitzhak Rabin in 1995. Amir was an ultra-Orthodox law student and follower of the teachings of Rabbi Avraham Isaac Kook and Zvi Yehuda Kook. As founders of the Hardal Religious Zionist movement, the Kooks emphasized strict observance and messianism. Their writings intimated that secular Jews, after building the state, would be forced to step aside so that the religious community would govern in accordance with biblical dictates. Nathan Zach, a well-known poet and publicist, wrote: "Because it warns of the upcoming holocaust, the [*Messiah's Donkey*] needs to be placed on every bookcase in Israel."[38]

Settler Violence

Rabbi Shlomo Min-Hahar, a leader of the Gush Emunim settler movement, became well-known for writing pocket books to spur military fervor among Israeli soldiers. He once described the entire Muslim world as "money-grubbing, despicable and capable of anything."[39] During the First Intifada, Shlomo Aviner, a leading rabbi in the Religious Zionist Movement, explicated Jewish law, or *Halacha,* to Jewish settlers, declaring:

As is known, no Halachic punishments can be inflicted upon Jewish boys below the age of thirteen and Jewish girls below the age of twelve. . . . Maimonides wrote that this rule applied to Jews alone. . . . Therefore, any non-Jews, no matter what age, will have to pay for any crime committed.[40]

Over the years, Israeli settler attacks against Palestinian civilians have escalated. In September 2008 a pipe bomb was detonated at the home of leftist Israeli professor Ze'ev Sternhell, injuring him slightly. Preceding the attacks, pamphlets had been distributed in his neighborhood by a group calling itself the Army of Liberators, offering a 1.1 million–shekel ($320,000) award to anyone who killed a member of the Peace Now movement, to which Professor Sternhell belonged. The pamphlet stated:

This country is ruled by a mob of wicked people, haters of the Torah, who want to erase the laws of God. . . . The state of Israel has become our enemy. . . . The time has come to set up a state of Jewish law in Judea and Samaria. The time has come for the Kingdom of Judea.[41]

Growing concerns of violence perpetrated by a new ultranationalist underground prompted Prime Minister Ehud Olmert to warn that "an evil wind of extremism, of hate, of maliciousness, of violence, of losing control, of lawbreaking, of contempt for the institutions of state, is passing through certain sections of the Israeli public."[42]

Israeli prosecutors determined that 502 criminal cases out of a total of 515 in 2007 involved right wing Jewish settlers in the Occupied Territories. A form of vigilantism has evolved within this community, employing a strategy known as "the price tag." It involves violent retaliation against Palestinians or Israeli government efforts perceived as challenging Jewish settlements in the West Bank, thus raising the human and financial costs incurred in dismantling any such communities.

While the violence perpetrated by settler extremists pales in comparison to lethal attacks by radical Palestinian groups, Israeli security officials worry that this underground movement is picking up steam and reenergizing the Jewish terrorist network responsible for plotting to blow up the Dome of the Rock Mosque in the early 1980s and killing a Peace Now activist in 1983. Israeli officials also fear that "unchecked settler violence could spark a new Palestinian intifada, enrage the Muslim world, and compromise Israel's international standing."[43]

In his 2004 article in *The New Yorker* called "Among the Settlers: Will They Destroy Israel?" Jeffrey Goldberg wrote:

> The most hard-core settlers are impatient messianists, who profess indifference, even scorn, for the state; a faith in vigilantism; and loathing for the Arabs. They are free of doubt, seeing themselves as taking orders from God, and are an unusually cohesive segment of Israeli society. Hard-core settlers and their supporters make up perhaps two per cent of the Israeli populace, but they nevertheless have driven Israeli policy in the occupied territories for much of the past thirty years.[44]

The Masada Complex

The more the outside world criticizes Israel's handling of the Palestinian problem, the more paranoid and distrustful Jews become, not just of Arabs and Muslims, but of the larger world as well. The psychological isolation that many Israelis suffer has increasingly bred interpretations of all international disapproval of the nation's policies as more evidence of a dangerous, anti-Semitic world bent on destroying the Jewish state.[45] It has even prompted discussions in some Jewish circles of patriotic suicide. In 1979 the American journalist Milton Viorst warned:

> Many Israelis these days speak, with some mixture of respect and dismay, of the nation's "Masada complex." I think they use the term to mean a fight-to-the-death courage as the enemy closes in around them. But there is a hint in the term that Israel, touched by some hysteria, is setting events on a course that makes a Masada-like outcome nearly inevitable. No doubt there is something pure, heroic, even incorruptible about Masada, and about the current Judaic resurgence. But as long as this spirit governs Israel it is difficult to see how there can be peace.[46]

A first-century CE Jewish historian named Flavius Josephus recorded the story of the heroic last stand of the Jews against the Roman Empire at Masada. After a two- to three- month siege, when the Roman soldiers finally breached the wall of the fortress from which the Jews fought, they found 936 dead bodies. Because their religion discouraged suicide, the Jews, who belonged to a sect known as the Zealots, were said to have killed one another in turn so that only the last one standing committed the sacrilege of suicide.

Israeli school children visit this historic site as part of the national curriculum. Some IDF units even hold their induction ceremonies for new soldiers there, replete with the oath that "Masada shall not fall again."

6

Burn out

In 2008 Israel celebrated its sixtieth birthday with some fanfare, some sadness, and much reflection. On the surface, Israeli society functions well. The Jewish state has much to be proud of, including world-class universities, a well-educated citizenry, a vibrant urban culture, a free press, and a democratic political culture. But personal grief for the casualties of incessant warfare cannot help but touch most families in so small a population. It is an economically viable society on the verge of emotional collapse.

From the moment of its founding in 1948, Israel has fought seven major wars and countless skirmishes. Between declared wars, 482 Israelis have died in suicide bombing attacks at shopping malls, on buses, and at cafés, pizzerias, and restaurants. Its citizens have adjusted their everyday lives to the unexpected and to the ever-present threat of new hostilities. But Israelis could not fail to notice that over the years, the Arabs have grown stronger in military organization and high-tech sophistication. The ranks of young recruits and suicide bombers have swelled. And Israeli Jews may be suffering a crisis of confidence in their ability to counter all future military threats. In a May 2008 article Jeffrey Goldberg wrote: "Our army is big, we have this atom bomb, but the inner feeling is of absolute fragility, that all the time we are at the edge of the abyss."[1]

In fact, political observers have described one of Israel's principal motives for the December 2008 invasion of Gaza as restoring Israel's deterrence—its ability to frighten its Arab neighbors from using aggression against it. However, a February 2009 article in the *Christian Science Monitor* also noted:

> While [Israel's] military superiority in the past has dealt crushing blows to Arab conventional armies, Israel has struggled to find a means of deterring a new generation of enemies, the smaller sub-state guerrilla movements exemplified by Hezbollah and Hamas. "These guys are not intimidated by the Israelis," says Timur Goksel, former senior official with the UN peacekeeping force in south Lebanon. "They are ideologically driven and don't have the same responsibilities as a state."[2]

The Laager Mentality

An Israeli psychotherapist living in Australia, Avigail Abarbanel, has described the mind-set of Israelis who find themselves trapped in a fearful worldview:

> This idea that Israel is the only safe place for Jews is critical to understanding the roots of the Palestinian-Israeli conflict, and Israel's policies and perspective in the present. The majority of Jewish people do not trust non-Jews as life-long compatriots. Experience and cultural narrative have been telling them that since antiquity, rulers and governments as well as populations have become hostile to Jews without warning. This means that no matter how long Jews have lived anywhere, no matter how unobtrusive and well integrated they have been, or how much they contributed to their society, things could turn against them overnight.[3]

Doctor Abarbanel added:

> With a history of European persecutions, pogroms, discriminatory laws, expulsions, medieval and modern ghettos and a systematic plan of total annihilation in what was considered an enlightened European country, it's hard to blame people for feeling insecure.[4]

The notion of a laager mentality was first used to describe the Afrikaners in South Africa who set out from the British Cape Colony in search of their own promised land in the hinterland. They circled their wagons into a laager to defend themselves from the threat of siege by hostile natives. These feelings of besiegement became a way of life and nourished the apartheid movement.

Dr. H. F. Stein has traced this siege mentality among Israelis back to the Holocaust, not as a single "grim event," but as "a metaphor for Jewish history itself."[5] Amos Elon, author of *The Israelis: Founders and Sons*, observed:

> The Holocaust remains a basic trauma of Israeli society. It is impossible to exaggerate its effect on the process of nation-building. . . . There is a latent hysteria in Israeli life that stems directly from this source. . . . The trauma of the Holocaust leaves an indelible mark on the national psychology, the tenor and content of public life, the conduct of foreign affairs, on politics, education, literature and the arts.[6]

Professor Daniel Bar-Tal of Tel Aviv University has warned that the siege or laager mentality can have dire consequences for Israel. They include:

1. The threatened society with siege beliefs develops negative attitudes towards other societies, which may be accompanied with feelings of xenophobia and chauvinism.
2. The society becomes extremely sensitive to any information and cues transmitted by other societies that may indicate negative intentions. This developed sensitivity is based on lack of trust and suspicion that society members feel toward other societies which, in their view, have negative intentions.
3. The society develops internal mechanisms to cope with the threat by increasing pressure among society members towards conformity, unity, and mobilization. This pressure can take various forms, like calls for unity, calls for patching-up or concealment of disagreement within the group, as well as threatening (and carrying out) negative sanctions against those who disagree within the group.

4. Finally, a society may take a course of action without consideration of international behavioral codes. A society that feels endangered may decide that its need to survive is so paramount that all means can be used. As a result, it may decide to take a course of action considered extreme and unacceptable by the international community. In this situation, society members may disregard any unfavorable reactions from these other groups, which they consider as their adversaries anyway.[7]

In a 1993 *Haaretz* article Doron Rosenblum offered an analysis of why this rhetoric has nevertheless been so persuasive:

> The suspicion is long-standing that members of the national camps [that is, the secular right] use power-mad rhetoric to cover their subliminal existential fear of the entire world. This fear was not dispelled in the slightest when the state of Israel was founded. Labor, in spite of all its faults, has succeeded by whatever means to cast aside such fear and replace it with a constructive and pragmatic world outlook. Likud, which resumed its historical note with ease, has not.[8]

In the fall of 2008 Avraham Burg came out with *The Holocaust Is Over: We Must Rise from its Ashes*. The Holocaust, he believes, has so traumatized Israelis that they find themselves in a situation where their nation is unable to "trust itself, its neighbors or the world around it."

Post-Traumatic Stress Disorder (PTSD)
Just as individuals can suffer chronic symptoms brought on by traumatic events, whole nations can also feel its effects in times of war. In their article, "The Persistence of War," Dr. Loren Cobb and Barbara F. Cobb declared:

> It is reasonable to suppose that if a large majority of the population suffers from PTSD and attachment disorders, then there will be serious consequences for all social institutions. The specific individual symptoms most likely to affect institutions are hypervigilance, emotional numbing, dissociation, denial, and apocalyptic thinking (PTSD), and the diminished capacity for empathy (AD).[9]

Israel is a society founded by those who had already suffered the emotional damage caused by the slaughter of nearly one-third of world Jewry in the Holocaust. David Eshel, an IDF veteran and writer, has called Israel and Gaza a "perfect laboratory" for the study of PTSD on account of suicide bombings, rocket attacks, and periodic war. An individual's symptoms may include flashbacks, nightmares, avoidant behavior, panic attacks, and unexplained irritability. Writing in the January 6, 2007, issue of *Defense Update News Analysis*, Eshel observed that many of the children and families suffering from PTSD in the southern Israeli town of Siderot "are not receiving any treatment simply because they fear leaving their homes and being struck by a Qassam rocket."[10]

An ultra-orthodox Jewish organization called Chesed Shel Emet (True Mercy) dispatches its well-trained volunteers to the scene of attacks. Their tasks are to "search and collect limbs and scrape down buildings splattered with blood and strips of flesh blown away by the blast of the explosion."[11] In this way, they try to ensure that the victims' entire body will receive a proper Jewish burial on the day of death. But, not surprisingly, members of Chesed Shel Emet suffer some of the most severe symptoms of PTSD.[12]

In *The Jewish Magazine* Yeshara Gold described one Jerusalem woman's experience:

> Aviva was just a block from the bookstore with her daughter's new school list in her pocket, when without warning, intense emotions welled up within her. "It wasn't fear that gripped me," she later explained, "but an overwhelming sadness as I walked on Jerusalem's Ben Yehuda Street. Tears flowed down my face as I passed my intended destination and found myself, instead standing outside the Ramon Cafe, a popular restaurant that had recently become once more the scene of violent death for Israelis." Aviva was never in a terrorist attack, nor was any member of her immediate family. But this young mother can be counted as one of the walking wounded, a Post Traumatic Stress Disorder (PTSD) casualty of this war.[13]

Medical researchers, in a February 2008 study of risk and resiliency factors among Jews and Arabs in Israel, reported that 6.6 percent of Jews and 18 percent of Arabs exposed to terrorist incidents suffered from PTSD.[14]

For residents of Sderot, on the border with Gaza, the statistics are much higher. A report in the *Jerusalem Post* stated:

> Even if you brandish statistics that never make the foreign media—like the fact that in Sderot, 28 percent of adults and 30 percent of children suffer from post-traumatic stress disorder, and more than 75 percent of children display some symptoms of post-traumatic stress—it makes little impression. Most people can imagine death, but they cannot imagine the slow erosion of life with a PTSD child who refuses to leave home for fear of rockets.[15]

Draft Dodgers and Blood Sacrifice

Adults generally accept the militarized nature of life in the Jewish state as an unfortunate necessity. However, a growing number of young Israelis have begun to argue that the altar of Zionism is demanding too much blood sacrifice. In his 2006 book, *Walled: Israeli Society at an Impasse*, Sylvain Cypel identified desertion from the military and draft evasion as being at an all-time high. The author noted: "The number of people seeking a thousand ways to escape the draft is increasing rapidly, a new phenomenon in a country in which military service has always been both a duty and a certificate of entry into active life."[16]

Aviv Geffen, a rock star and great-nephew of Israeli military leader and politician Moshe Dayan, openly admitted he "avoided army service by threatening suicide if he were enlisted."[17] In 2007 the Israeli government initiated a "shaming campaign" in which popular singers and other young entertainers who had failed to complete the nation's mandatory military service requirement were banned from holding concerts and making television appearances. The military has also begun cracking down on those whom they believe fake mental illness to evade being drafted. The number of potential draftees who "fail" psychological tests are at an all-time high of 5 percent for males and 3 percent for females.[18]

In 1987 a group of high-school age conscientious objectors was formed that called itself Shministim, which means twelfth-graders. By 2008 more than 3,000 Israeli high school students belonged to that organization, and all have been threatened with jail time for refusing to serve in the military. Another group of peace activists organized the New Profile movement in 1998 to encourage conscientious objections and other acts of refusal to perform military service. In January 2002, 51 reserve soldiers and officers signed what came to be known as the Courage to Refuse Letter, in which they accepted military service but refused to serve in the Occupied Territories, declaring their unwillingness "to fight beyond the 1967 borders in order to dominate, expel, starve, and humiliate an entire people."[19] By 2008 the number of signatories had risen to 633. As of the same year, 52 IDF reservists had refused military service, as had members of two elite military units.[20]

Military Exhaustion

Studies have also shown that the number one cause of death among Israeli soldiers is suicide. An article in the July 15, 2004, *Ma'ariv International* cited statistics from the Israeli army's rehabilitation division and noted that the number of suicide deaths among IDF troops in 2003 was higher than the 43 soldiers killed in battle that year.[21]

In the spring of 2001 Professor Eyal Zisser of Tel Aviv University wrote an article in *The Middle East Quarterly* identifying "Israel's exhaustion" as an important factor in eroding the Jewish state's strategic deterrence. Zisser declared:

> The new Palestinian violence has caused some important voices in the Israeli public to call for their government to accept, in essence, all of the Palestinians' demands (withdrawal to the June 1967 border line; the break-up of most, if not all, West Bank and Gaza settlements; the establishment of an independent Palestinian state; and a solution to the question of refugees acceptable to Palestinians). This readiness to accede to Palestinian demands has its roots in a physical and psychological exhaustion—weariness of the on-going conflict and a lack of conviction in the rightness of the Israeli position.[22]

Professor Zisser added:

> Many military analysts make the error of relying too much on capabilities. They pit soldier against soldier, tank against tank, and pay too much attention to the qualitative and technological difference between Israel and the Arabs. While these quantitative and qualitative data are a component of military strength, they are not the sole consideration.

One must also add such factors as attitudes toward the potential enemy, will and determination, commitment, national unity, readiness for sacrifice, and public consensus. Whatever Israel's advantage over the Arabs in hardware, it is clearly weaker in the area of software.[23]

Literature in Mourning

Some of the most common themes in contemporary Israeli literature involve the decay and death of the state. Amos Oz's most noted novel, *My Michael*, presents the portrait of a young woman whose mental breakdown was mirrored in an atmosphere of "brooding insanity and illness" within Jerusalem itself. Virtually all of the novels of A. B. Yehoshua have treated the question of Israel's future. His bestselling novel *The Lover* told the story of an IDF soldier who suddenly lost faith in what he was fighting for and of an Israeli girl from a well-to-do family who took an Arab lover.

Yoram Hazony, a noted Zionist political theorist, has lamented the common narrative in contemporary Israeli literature, defined as ". . . the escape from Israel; the destruction of Israel; death (by decay, rather than struggle); the Israel Defense Forces as concentration camp, pigsty, whorehouse; and the ideal of disempowerment represented by the Holocaust."[24] Hazony added:

> Israel is in the midst of an ideological disintegration whose magnitude and meaning defy comprehension. Its most prominent political and cultural figures speak about the absorption of the country into the Arab League, [and] compare the Israeli armed forces to Nazis. . . .[25]

According to the Israeli-born, American scholar Meyrav Wurmser, "Sephardic writers like Sami Michael, Yitzhak Gormazano-Goren, and Albert Swissa portray the Sephardic Jew as an Arab-Jew who, like his Arab brothers, suffered under the yoke of white (Ashkenazi) colonialism."[26] To prove her point, Professor Wurmser cites a poem by the popular Israeli poet Aharon Shabtai:

> *Already from the window of the parked airplane one can*
> *see that we have returned to the same excrement from*
> *which we came.*
> *But to complain, to lament, to cry,*

*Is only a part of the tax-package required of the educated
citizen. The country's corrupt, dishonorable and stuttering
rulers want the freezer to be filled with delicate literary
meat. Therefore, I propose to shorten the soul to a line that
connects between two points:
A. To know that there is no difference between Yitzhak
Rabin and Benjamin Netanyahu . . .
B. The poet, the intellectual, is not one who reads Kafka
or Marcel Proust when liberty and justice are being
trampled on in the markets. No, in a forever-young body
he stands, lowering his pants, and urinates on the dying
bonfire of Zionism. . . .[27]*

Corruption

One of the most telling ways the stresses of Israeli life play themselves out is in corruption scandals, which BBC reporter Martin Patience has called an "epidemic" in that society.[28] In September 2008 Prime Minister Ehud Olmert stepped down over allegations that he had submitted duplicate and in some cases even triplicate bills for travel expenses. Another scandal involved his "steering tens of millions of pounds' worth of state funds towards a company owned by his former law partner, Uri Messer, and unlawfully accepted cash-stuffed envelopes from a U.S. businessman."[29] In June 2008 the former president of Israel Moshe Katsav was charged with rape and sexual harassment of female employees.

A November 2008 article in the Israeli daily *Haaretz* reported that 72 percent of the Israeli public believed the nation was "rife with corruption." The article quoted Maj. Gen. Uzi Dayan, president of the Sderot Conference for Society, who declared: "the corruption of state institutions is the primary factor preventing them from taking pride in their country."[30]

It is not altogether clear whether corruption has grown or whether more focus is being paid to the shady dealings of politicians and financiers. In 1983 nearly one-fifth of the Israeli population learned that their fast-growing bank shares were, in effect, a giant Ponzi scheme. Investors were being paid not by the actual returns on their investment but by the fresh money being brought in as new investors were attracted to what appeared to be unusually profitable stock. Corrupt bankers had used deposits funds illegally borrowed through shady offshore subsidiaries, which allowed some shares to increase 1 to 2 percent daily. When the crash came, the Israeli government was forced to nationalize the banking industry and compensate shareholders at a cost of 15 percent of the nation's gross national product (GNP).

Daniel Kayros, spokesman for the Movement for Quality Governant in Israel, attributed corruption to the Israeli public's focus on security issues. He stated: "You may be committed to other social issues but in this country the security issues trump everything."[31] An anticorruption group based in Berlin, Germany, said that Israel had slipped three places in its annual "Corruptions Perceptions Index" in the past year and in 2008 sat in thirty-third place between Dominica and the United Arab Emirates.[32]

An Insurance Policy

Jewish law from ancient times set certain restrictions on leaving Israel; namely, it was only allowable under conditions of famine. During the early days of the modern Israeli republic, *yerida*—Jewish emigration from Israel—was looked on with disdain. In a 1976 interview Prime Minister Rabin referred to such emigrants as "weaklings." However, in recent years the public reaction to emigration has mellowed as the numbers leaving have swelled and the negative term "yerida" diminished in usage.

In fact, Israel has been losing its most talented citizens at an alarming rate. Haviv Rettig, a reporter for the *Jerusalem Post*, observed: "The very best academic minds are fleeing to the United States and the United Kingdom like, well, rats from a sinking ship."[33] Rettig reported:

> Across all academic fields, Israel has a higher percentage of its researchers, 24.9%, living in America than any other country. The next-highest, Canada, has 12.2%. And Canada itself is an exception, with the next in line, the Netherlands, with 4.3% and Italy with 4.2%.[34]

In the technology field, Amir Ben-Artzi of *EE Times Israel* reported that the question has become ". . . why the latest world-class talents would want to live and work in a country in which wars break out every 10 years, governments are replaced every two years and political corruption is breaking records."[35]

As of 2004 there were 760,000 Israelis living abroad. Of those still residing in the Jewish state, many have applied for second country passports to the United States, Canada, the United Kingdom, France, and even Germany. All Israelis who can trace their ancestry to Europe, escaped the Nazis, or survived the Holocaust have been made eligible for European Union passports. In one year alone the German embassy in Tel Aviv issued more than 3,000 passports to Israelis. In fact, Germany boasted of having the fastest-growing population of Jews in Europe.[36] An even more recent survey conducted in 2008 by the Jerusalem-based Menachem Begin Heritage Center showed that 59 percent of Israelis possessed or were seeking passports from a second nation or information about obtaining foreign citizenship.

While economic considerations have motivated some, security concerns ranked foremost in the minds of most Israelis applying for second passports. It has even been suggested that Israeli Jews were using the possibility of emigrating, applying for and obtaining second passports from other countries, as a stress reliever to help them cope with the daily anxieties of living in a country plagued with endemic political violence. Sylvain Cypel asserted: "The race for European passports reveals an inexpressible lack of confidence in the future of the state such as it is."[37]

While a Gallup World Poll conducted in 2007 revealed that one-fifth of all Israelis wished that they could immigrate to another country, nearly half of Israeli teens between the ages of fourteen and eighteen "expressed a desire to relocate to another country." In an article entitled "The Parents Are Running the Country; the Children Are Overseas," a major Hebrew daily newspaper, *Yediot Ahronot,* reported:

> . . . the two sons of Minister Roni Milo (a right-wing moderate) were living in New York. Tali, daughter of Defense Minister Benyamin Ben Eliezer (a Labor hawk), was also in the United States. Yitzhak Rabin's son Yuval had settled in Washington. Orit, granddaughter of former prime minister Menachem Begin, had also left Israel. Ehud Barak had recently known the joy of becoming a grandfather; his daughter Michael had given birth in New York, where she lives with her husband. Ygal, the son of former defense minister Moshe Arens of Likud, lives in Los Angeles. The lawyer Yoel Herzog, son of former president Haim Herzog, had opted for Geneva. . . .[38]

Bernard Avishai, author of *The Tragedy of Zionism* and a consulting editor with the *Harvard Business Review,* said: ". . . About a third of forty-five business and law students [he] taught a few years ago at the Interdisciplinary Center, in Herzliya, now live abroad, and many of them may never return." Avishai added:

> Will the young people take the job offer in London from Goldman Sachs or will they stay here and wait for the missiles to fall? . . . The question is, is this a good enough place to come back to when they are married and have children? Finally, the Israeli government has to confront its own crazies and create a national consensus on democratic ideals, enact a secular constitution, and really confront the settlers.[39]

However, all Israelis are not bankers or the sons and daughters of wealthy politicians or nuclear physicists. Because of financial considerations, many Ashkenazic Jews cannot travel at will, even if they are able to obtain a second passport. As for Jews from the Middle East and Africa, they have no "escape clause" written into their Israeli passports.

7

Magical Thinking

In a July 2006 *Washington Post* article columnist Richard Cohen called Israel a "mistake." He said:

> It is an honest mistake, a well-intentioned mistake, a mistake for which no one is culpable, but the idea of creating a nation of European Jews in an area of Arab Muslims (and some Christians) has produced a century of warfare and terrorism of the sort we are seeing now.

But then Cohen concluded that despite these problems, "Israel is here to stay."[1] However, it is that piece of magical thinking that might turn out to be the most dangerous threat to Israeli Jews since the emergence of Palestinian nationalism. It would not be the first time the Jewish people miscalculated the intentions and strength of their enemy.

Denial

Israelis seeking second passports have no illusions about their country's future. But American and other supporters of the status quo in Israel may be engaging in a lethal form of denial. Bolkosky believed that they failed to recognize Hitler's intentions for two reasons. First, during the period before the outbreak of World War II, German Jews tended to dismiss anti-Semitic behavior on the part of their countrymen as excessive but harmless demonstrations of one's German patriotism. Thus Jews responded with greater professions of their own allegiance to Germany, which was the only home they knew. Second, this highly educated community of Jews embraced the expansive, tolerant values of the Enlightenment and believed that the German public did as well, not just a few of its more well-known philosophers.[2] Professor Peter Loewenberg of the University of California at Los Angeles also called this pre–World War II myth that was prevalent among Jews who had successfully assimilated into German culture as "fatally maladaptive" and "an exercise in self-deception." He noted: "Some myths may be constructive in presenting a vision of the world as it can become and thus motivate men to action. Others are illusory prescriptions for disaster."[3] Likewise, Theodore Hamerow, in *Why We Watched*, declared:

> Not only were [German Jews] reluctant to admit to themselves that they had been rejected by the nation of their birth, the nation of "thinkers and poets" to which most of them remained deeply attached, but many were also convinced that the Hitler dictatorship was a fleeting phenomenon, a brief aberration.[4]

Of course, the Holocaust disabused any lingering doubters of the myth of the assimilated "German Jew, to whom no harm would come." And yet we find this narrative of the Jewish people being saved from total destruction embedded within every layer of modern Israeli culture and society. Even American Jewish leaders talk of their history in terms of crises that they have pulled through "against all odds." But faith in Zionism as a secular religion is considerably more perilous than faith in the Bible, if only because the laws of human nature can be more ruthless even than an angry God.

In the fall of 2006 writer Tom Ivy produced a popular documentary, *Against All Odds: Israel Survives*, that was shown on Israeli television as well as the popular Christian Trinity Broadcasting Network in the United States. The program offered eyewitness accounts of miraculous rescues and supernatural phenomena that were believed to have contributed to the creation and survival of modern Israel. One vignette dramatized Israeli troops being saved by a mysterious wind, which exposed thousands of hidden land mines during the 1973 Yom Kippur War. Another depicted the life of Shula Cohen, a Jewish woman living in Beirut in 1948, who risked her life to become one of Israel's most important spies. Avigdor Kahalani, an Israeli soldier and politican, figured in yet another miracle narrative in which he narrowly escaped death in 1967. Then, six years later, he put together a brilliant battle plan that saved the young nation from the onslaught of a Syrian tank armada.

Some may scoff at the emotionalism displayed in the documentary, but many Israelis and supporters of Israel in the diaspora have nevertheless been seduced by the message. Chaim Herzog, who later became the sixth president of Israel, helped to instill this "miracle narrative" into secular Israeli society after the 1973 Yom Kippur War. In his book *The Terrible Days,* Herzog wrote about the Israeli people ". . .being saved miraculously, after escaping an attempt to destroy us." Professor Tirza Hechter, a lecturer in political science at Bar-Ilan University in Israel, asserts that Herzog served as "the national commentator" of the Yom Kippur War. It was he who framed the war and all its traumas for the Israeli public. Hechter asserts:

> According to Herzog's interpretation, it was not only the superior fighting of Israel's soldiers that helped them survive and overcome the mighty enemy attack. It was also because of the miracle in which many believed—a miracle in the sense of belonging to a nation in whose history miracles occurred when its people were in danger and threatened with destruction.[5]

In a 2005 interview Abraham Rabinovich, a *Jerusalem Post* reporter and author of *The Yom Kippur War: The Epic Encounter that Transformed the Middle East,* reinforces this miracle imagery:

> Within two weeks of its disastrous setback, the Israeli army was pounding on the gates of Damascus and threatening Cairo. I asked major historians like John Keegan and Donald Kagan whether they could think of any parallel in history, modern or ancient, in which an army, so badly mauled, had recovered and regained the initiative so quickly against such formidable odds. None of them could.[6]

All nations have their myths of exceptionalism, but few have ever faced the level of challenges to its survival that Israel now confronts. Myths bring people together, but in appealing to the emotions, they can sometimes paint illusions that disguise the distance to the edge of the cliff. It took the Soviet Union seventy years to emerge from the chrysalis of communist social engineers, spread its wings, soar to the heights of superpowerdom, and then crash, seemingly without warning. Having failed to meet the minimum economic needs of its citizens, its myths of exceptionalism ensured that the nation would be unprepared for the fate that awaited it.

Israel's diverse, technologically savvy economy is, in contrast, booming. In the last quarter of 2006 it grew at an astonishing 8 percent, according to Sever Plocker, one of Israel's top economic writers. Foreign direct investment is flowing into the country at an astonishing rate—$13.4 billion in 2006. The budget deficit is minuscule and the stock exchange is robust.[7] However, the goals that Israel set for itself are not the same as those of the former Soviet Union. Those Israeli goals—the creation of both a safe haven for the Jewish people and a liberal democracy in a territory shared with a hostile Arab minority—may simply be incompatible with longevity.

Permanent War

Israel cannot go on forever in a state of war. The more aggression it used to preempt its Arab neighbors, the more explosive became their resistance to the Jewish state. As Israeli novelist David Grossman once said:

> Now we must look . . . not to the familiar, instinctive reaction of the Israeli way of fighting—that is, what doesn't work with force will work with much more force.
>
> Force, in this case, will fan the flames of hatred for Israel in the region and the entire world, and may even, heaven forbid, create the situation that will bring upon us the next war and push the Middle East to an all-out, regional war. [8]

Much of Israel's strategy was based on belief in an eventual Arab acquiescence to the Jewish state in the face of Israel's overwhelming military power. But this attitude represented a profound misreading of Arab culture. The people of the desert knew how to wait. Israel's strategic dilemma was

compounded by the diversity of opinion among the nation's many political factions. The present government focused on the use of arbitrary road-
blocks, a suffocation of the Palestinian economy, and the building of a
436-mile-long security wall separating Jewish and Palestinian populations
on the borders of the West Bank. There have even been the intimations of
a possible war against Iran and Syria aimed at halting the transshipment of
weapons to the Hezbollah movement in Southern Lebanon. Dr. Daniel
Pipes, a political analyst who was also the founder and director of the
Middle East Forum, a Zionist think tank, recently asserted:

> Israelis eventually must gird themselves to resuming the difficult, bit-
> ter, long and expensive effort needed to convince the Palestinians and
> others that their dream of eliminating Israel is defunct. Should Israelis
> fail to achieve this, then Israel itself will be defunct.[9]

The more exhausted the Jewish state becomes, the more likely that
fanaticism rather than reason will dictate policy decisions. But Israeli strategists and their American neoconservative counterparts see things differ-
ently. Dr. Victor Davis Hanson, a senior fellow at the Hoover Institute,
uses examples from defeated fifth-century Athens, the Confederacy, and
Japan after World War II to assert:

> force . . . has a way of making people change. Even the most militant
> citizenries can be disabused of their rather dangerous ideas—but only after
> they understand that the logical consequences of their extremism are im-
> poverishment, ruin and humiliation. . . . Both our own war against the
> terrorists and the Israeli response on the West Bank—if conducted force-
> fully and coupled with the clear intention to help the defeated to rebuild
> their societies—can prompt real peace rather than breed endless war.[10]

This strategy presupposes that the war is winnable in Israel's favor. The
Jewish state's iron wall strategy of creating military invincibility did not
take into account the agency of those displaced by its nationhood. The
Israelis have been unfairly accused of morphing into Nazis and plotting
genocide against the Palestinians, but Israel's biggest problem was that genocide was never an option. Even had the Jews lost their moorings and sunk
to the level of colonial America or seventeenth-century South Africa, the

Palestinians were not an aboriginal people. Millions of them could not have been "disposed of" using measles-contaminated blankets. And the Palestinian tribesmen on horseback and camels, whom the early Zionists faced years ago, are not the Palestinians battling Israel in the early twenty-first century. They have been replaced by men and women who are organized, disciplined, and using the most sophisticated weaponry available on the international arms market.

Even during intervals of relative peace, Israel has found itself hemmed in by threats in all directions. On its northern border with Lebanon, it has confronted the radical Islamist group, Hezbollah, which the Israeli army was unable to dislodge from its strongholds during the 2006 war with Lebanon. Syria, sitting on Israel's northeast border, remains in a state of war with the Jewish state and has been accused of following Iran's lead in working clandestinely to establish a nuclear weapons capability. In February 2009 *Haaretz* also reported: "Syria has stepped up production of its chemical weapons."[11] That report was based on research published on *Jane's Defence News* website. According to an earlier *Times* (London) article, a 2007 Israeli commando raid on a secret Syrian military installation turned up weapons-grade nuclear material of North Korean origin.[12]

The occupied West Bank of the Jordan River sits on Israel's eastern boundary. With a population of 2.5 million Palestinians, it has been a staging area for terrorist attacks and political unrest. Gaza, on Israel's western border, is the Jewish state's most volatile neighbor. It is home to nearly 500,000 Palestinians and is led by the militant Islamic Hamas Party, which has vowed to destroy Israel. Barry Rubin, director of the Global Research in International Affairs Center, offers a sobering assessment of the situation:

> There is no solution; the enemy is not going away, nor will it moderate. The world wants to hear that Israel is seeking peace and doing everything possible, and it will. Yet while attacks can be deterred, reduced in number and made less effective, actual peace is beyond reach.[13]

America's Strategic Dead End
Israel's only real ally, the United States, has become so exhausted by the ill-conceived war in Iraq that it has neither the military wherewithal nor the diplomatic influence to protect Israel in any meaningful way. More important, the American Israel Public Affairs Committee (AIPAC) and its

neoconservative supporters are now on the defensive, being blamed for the Iraq invasion in the first place.[14] U.S. policy toward Israel is not only dangerous for the long-term interests of Jews, it also harms America's own strategic interests in the region.

While former U.S. Representative Henry Hyde has called for a "Marshall Plan" for Palestinian Arabs, perhaps to buy them off, Israel's far right advocates evicting the Palestinian Arabs from the West Bank and Gaza. They also talk of clearing southern Lebanon of its indigenous population in order to create a buffer zone of safety.

But if one stands back from the fray and merely observes, the troubling quality of all this is that the existence of the Jewish state is getting more perilous rather than less. The real question in the Middle East today is how far Israelis are willing to go in order to retain the Jewishness of their increasingly Arab-populated state. Will Israelis have to abandon morality, their sense of justice, and the principles of liberal democracy for the sake of the Jewish state? And whatever they do, are they just buying time as their enemies grow demographically larger and militarily more sophisticated?

Some Zionists have turned to Canadian political philosopher Will Kymlicka for guidance. They interpret him as arguing in *Liberalism, Community and Culture* that even in a liberal democratic state it is sometimes necessary to exercise coercion and deny basic freedoms to groups that might threaten its overall functioning.[15] In an essay entitled "When Magical Thinking Will Not Suffice: Israeli Democracy, Israeli Arabs and the Kinneret Agreement," writer Daniel Gordis asserts that Israel must begin to make tough choices. He suggests creating a Galilean Triangle in which the areas of Israel that are most highly populated by Palestinian Arabs have their citizenship taken away in order that they be annexed to a Palestinian homeland. It would be difficult to imagine this stop-gap solution as creating anything other than an ungovernable Arab Bantustan, even though for electoral purposes it would reduce the Palestinian population within Israel proper. If that is too unpalatable for the Israeli electorate, Gordis suggests that Israelis give serious consideration to limiting the concept of liberal democracy so as to preserve the Jewish nature of the majority Israeli electorate.[16]

In "Does Israel Need a Plan?" Doctor Pipes identifies a laundry list of proposals under discussion, including the offering of financial inducements to Arab-Israeli citizens and Palestinians in the West Bank and Gaza to immigrate to Egypt or Jordan. But if that doesn't work, involuntary transfers can be undertaken. Pipes, however, does not endorse either of these courses of action. Rather, he insists that Israel "can and must win decisively," presumably on the battlefield (an easy enough proposal for an Israeli supporter commuting between Cambridge, Massachusetts, and Philadelphia, Pennsylvania).[17]

International Terrorism

Israel is not to blame for the September 11, 2001, attacks on the World Trade Center and the Pentagon; the 2002 bomb blast in Bali, which killed 180 civilians; or the 2008 Mumbai attack, which killed 188 people. These acts were the work of an interlocking global terrorist network. While the mastermind behind the U.S. attacks, Osama bin Laden, has condemned American support for Israeli policy toward the Palestinians, the plight of these Arabs appear to be little more than a smokescreen for bin Laden's deeper preoccupation with the conservative rulers of his own country of Saudi Arabia and their collusion with the United States. The root causes of terrorism are complex. Dr. Akiko Fukushima, the director of policy studies at the Japanese National Institute for Research Advancement, has said: "When a sense of injustice and inequality, be it poverty, access to politics, resources or other grievances, cannot be resolved through proper channels of governance, it may spur people to more violent resolutions out of desperation, including terrorism."[18]

Nevertheless, it is true that the rise of fundamentalist Islam after the 1967 Six-Day War became an unintended consequence of the Arabs' humiliating loss of territory at the hands of the IDF. This collapse of the secular pan-Arabism, represented by the militarily weak Arab governments, opened the door to a radicalized and intensely political form of Islam. In transcending ethnicity, it appealed to a potential audience in the billions, including Iranians, Pakistanis, Indonesians, and other non-Arab Muslims.

International terrorism is like gangrene. Its opportunistic toxins seek out suppurative wounds in the political landscape caused by endemic conflict and unresolved grievances. Professor Mearsheimer and Professor Walt asserted:

> Support for Israel is not the only source of anti-American terrorism,
> but it is an important one, and it makes winning the war on terror

more difficult. . . . Unconditional support for Israel makes it easier for extremists to rally popular support and to attract recruits.[19]

Zionism, seen as a Western colonialist enterprise, and the Palestinian-Israel conflict fuel the rage of its adherents and serve as recruiting mechanisms for its underground cells and militias. The U.S. invasion of Iraq, pushed by Zionist neo-conservatives, only worsened matters.

Failing Two-State Approach
With catchy names like the Camp David Accords, the Oslo Accords, the Clinton Parameters, and the Roadmap for Peace, Israel has, in sixty-plus years of existence, cobbled together innumerable peace plans with its Arab neighbors. But there is no peace, only intermittent lulls in a perpetual war.

The Oslo Accords of 1993 promised to be the breakthrough that everyone had been hoping for once it became clear that the 1978 Camp David Accords had only shifted the locus of hostilities from threats of an Egyptian invasion to Palestinian uprisings within the Israeli heartland itself. In the agreement signed in Oslo, Norway, on August 20, 1993, by Prime Minister Rabin and Yasser Arafat of the PLO, the Palestinians did recognize Israel's right to exist. The Olso Accords hinted at a "two-state solution," in which the Palestinians living in the Occupied Territories would be given their own independent state.

But on February 25, 1994, Baruch Goldstein, an Israeli-American settler, attacked a group of Muslim worshippers praying at a mosque in Hebron, killing 29 and wounding 125. A year later, Yigal Amir, another ultra-orthodox Jew enraged by the Oslo peace initiative, assassinated Prime Minister Rabin. As relations between Israelis and Palestinians deteriorated, two spontaneous uprisings erupted in the Occupied Territories. When Hamas won the Palestinian elections in 2006, it immediately repudiated the Oslo Accords, refusing either to recognize Israel's right to exist or to renounce violence.

In November 2007 the United States sponsored a Middle East peace conference in Annapolis, Maryland, in which the government of Israel and the Palestinian Authority agreed for the first time to a two-state solution in practice rather than merely in principle as had occurred in Oslo fourteen years before. Even before the conference had convened, Immanuel

Wallerstein, a U.S. sociologist, was calling it the "last call for a two-state solution." He asked in a November 2007 *International Herald Tribune* column: "Why the tone of desperation?" His answer was:

> . . . the 20th century international consensus on the two-state solution
> is fading away. . . Sympathy for Israel, once so strong, is declining even
> in quarters once strongly sympathetic to the Israeli position, and with
> this there are increased calls for a unitary state.[20]

Israelis are divided on the issue. Benjamin Netanyahu, who was elected prime minister in 2009, has insisted that any two-state solution must limit Palestinian sovereignty in matters of defense and weapons acquisition so that it is not able to threaten Israel's existence. The Hamas Party came to power in Gaza in 2006, sending shivers of trepidation throughout Jewish society. The Israeli government responded to the new threat by reinforcing its matrix of control over the Occupied Territories. Israeli-American anthropologist Jeff Halper identifies two components of this plan. He refers to the first component as creating "Facts on the Ground." This includes expropriation of land—including threats, extortion and bribes on Palestinians to sell their lands—and the carving up of the Occupied Territories in ways that "do not permit freedom of movement" in certain areas and "restricted housing in Palestinian East Jerusalem." Professor Halper also includes the construction of a system of highways and bypass roads "to link settlements and create barriers between Palestinian areas" and to "control movement through the imposition of closed military areas, establishing a thick web of internal checkpoints and maintaining control of all border crossings." The Israelis also control water rights and other natural resources vital to the functioning of the Palestinian territories.[21]

Professor Halper has asserted that the second component of Israeli control over the Palestinian areas is through a "Web of Bureaucracy," in which government officials of the Jewish state:

1. "Close" the West Bank and Gaza permanently, thereby violating freedom of movement and goods, impoverishing the Palestinian population and destroying the Palestinian economy.
2. Issue permits restricting freedom of movement both within the country and abroad.

3. Zone land so as to freeze the natural development of Palestinian towns and villages. Building permits, enforced by house demolitions, arrests, fines and daily harassment, work well.
4. Draw expansive "master plans" around settlements, and then claim that settlement building has been "frozen."
5. Restrict planting of crops. Destroy others, like the hundreds of thousands of olive and fruit trees uprooted since 1967.
6. Employ licensing and inspection of Palestinian businesses as a means of political control.[22]

In August 2004 Daniel Seidemann, an Israeli lawyer, penned the article "Letting Israel Self-Destruct" for the *Washington Post* in which he warned that Israel's construction of a security wall that cuts East Jerusalem off from the Palestinians will rule out:

> the possibility of East Jerusalem ever becoming the national seat of Palestine. Given the topography, it will dismember the West Bank into two cantons, with no natural connection between them. If implemented, the plan will create a critical mass of facts on the ground that will render nearly impossible the creation of a sustainable Palestinian state with any semblance of geographical integrity. . . . Dovetailed with settlement activity, it threatens to create the critical mass of political fact that further undermines the feasibility of the two-state solution.[23]

A United Nations report published in 2007 found:

> 38 percent of the West Bank is now taken up by Israeli infrastructure—roads, settlements, military bases and so on—largely off-limits to Palestinians. Israel has methodically broken the remainder of the territory into dozens of enclaves separated from each other and the outside world by zones that it alone controls (including, at last count), 6123 checkpoints and roadblocks.[24]

In short, Israel exercises control over nearly half of the territory that is supposed to constitute the Palestinian state. So why are Israelis so reluctant to grant full autonomy to the Occupied Territories? One reason is that Hamas, which controls Gaza, refuses to recognize the Jewish state of Israel and backs up its refusal with near-daily rocket attacks into Israel.

In October 2008 the Israelis were once again discussing a peace plan first issued by the Saudi Arabian government in 2002. The plan called for the return of land seized during the 1967 war, including the West Bank, Golan Heights, Gaza Strip, and East Jerusalem, in exchange for peace. But on December 27, Israeli forces launched a major attack on Hamas military and political targets in Gaza in retaliation for Hamas rockets being fired on southern Israel. The war complicated Israel's relationships with the moderate Arab states because of an upsurge in support for Hamas on the Arab street as gruesome photographs of dead and injured Palestinian women and children circulated in the media and on the Internet. Some observers now fear that Israel may have unwittingly accomplished what 1,300 years of history was unable to do, unify Shiite and Sunni factions against a common enemy—the Jewish state.

Echoes of South Africa

Israelis are right to wince at those who question their right to exist. And yet, the more meaningful query is not about which states have the right to exist. It is whether Israel, after more than sixty years, has indeed become a fait accompli? This is where the case of South Africa becomes instructive. In 2006 President Jimmy Carter published his controversial book, *Palestine: Peace Not Apartheid*. He declared:

> A system of apartheid, with two peoples occupying the same land but completely separated from each other, with Israelis totally dominant and suppressing violence by depriving Palestinians of their basic human rights. This is the policy now being followed, although many citizens of Israel deride the racist connotation of prescribing permanent second-class status for the Palestinians.[25]

Even before the book came out, a vigorous debate had erupted as to whether Israel and South Africa were similar cases. As early as 2000, the description of Israel as an "emerging apartheid state" was being heard in some international circles. In August–September 2001, a UN antiracism conference of nongovernmental organizations in Durban, South Africa, adopted resolutions denouncing Israel an "apartheid state," calling for international sanctions and resurrecting a 1975 UN resolution that had since been rescinded condemning Zionism as racism.[26]

In South Africa, the economic lives of blacks and whites were deeply intertwined. The economic viability of South Africa was contingent on cheap black labor. Likewise, the Palestinian and Jewish populations are interconnected, although not to the same degree. Even though Arabs universally denounce Jewish settlements in the Occupied Territories, an estimated 25 percent of all Palestinian workers are employed in the Jewish settlements in the West Bank and East Jerusalem.[27]

So fearful were South African leaders of whites being murdered in their sleep by black communist insurgents that the apartheid regime launched a secret nuclear weapons program in the 1970s.[28] In the case of South Africa, growing international pressure pushed the apartheid regime to dismantle the system of strict racial separation and its paranoia-fueled nuclear weapons program. There is no such international consensus regarding Israel and the Palestinians. However, as Ali Abunimah, a Palestinian-American reporter and author of *One Country*, has pointed out:

> . . . the European and American governments were not eager to put sanctions on South Africans—they had a lot of good business with them. It was a civil society movement, very much ad hoc on campuses and churches that eventually forced governments to put sanctions in place.[29]

In the early 1990s South Africa had the most successful economy in Africa. No one, neither the most astute international observers nor the South Africans themselves foresaw the sudden collapse of the apartheid regime. Even though international sanctions and black protests played a role, South Africa for the most part collapsed from within. The South African government lost legitimacy among whites. They were tired of the isolation, tired of fighting, and tired of hauling around the cultural baggage dictated by the theology of apartheid. And yet, South Africa did not vanish from the map. It evolved into a stable, multiracial democracy.

When Yoram Hazony writes a book called *The Jewish State: The Struggle for Israel's Soul* and spends 400 pages decrying the de-Judaization of Israeli society, Israel's trajectory does indeed begin to sound like South Africa's before the collapse of apartheid. In the book's introduction, entitled "The

Jewish State Doesn't Live Here Anymore," Hazony makes the following lament:

> In the Education Ministry, the chairman of a committee revising the public-school history curriculum announced that the Jewish people would be included in the new curriculum, "But certainly not as a subject of primary importance;" in the Defense Ministry, an official code of values and principles was approved for training Israeli soldiers in which the Jewish people and the Jewish state are not even mentioned; on the Supreme Court, the chief justice had devised a new constitutional doctrine whereby the "Jewish" character of the state had to be interpreted "at the highest level of abstraction" so that it became identical with the universal dictates of what is acceptable in any generic democracy; prominent officials and public figures had begun to talk of changing the Israeli national anthem (to remove the words "Jewish soul") and repealing the Law of Return (so that diaspora Jews would no longer have a right to immigrate to Israel)—and so on.[30]

Hazony adds:

> When one considers all of these examples and others, it is impossible to escape the conclusion that Israel's public culture is undergoing a massive shift away from the ideas and norms that characterized it as a Jewish state—a very broad phenomenon that in the last few years has received the name "post-Zionism."[31]

Hazony blames the Israeli intellectual and cultural elite for this state of affairs. Ironically, he insists that what Israel needs most are new ideas. But in truth he has overlooked the most powerful new ideas being articulated across the Israeli spectrum simply because they do not fit his neatly packaged Zionist paradigm.

And the true analogy with South Africa is in recognition of the fact that, as Ernest Renan says, "a nation's existence is . . . a daily plebiscite, just as an individual's existence is a perpetual affirmation of life."[32] When the consensus breaks down, the nation unravels, whatever its economic strength. Most scholarly observers believe that in the case of South Africa, the question became to what lengths were white South Africans willing to go to maintain the "whiteness" of their government and their own special privileges? The answer was that after forty-five years, the whole enterprise finally became too exhausting.

8

A Cacophony of Zions

Zionism's accomplishments have been myriad and impressive, including the fact that nearly six million Jews speak, write, and produce literature in a tongue that moldered in the cemetery of dead languages for 2,000 years. But what it has not been able to do is change the trajectory of impending doom that hovers over the Jewish people. A plethora of new Zionisms has emerged since Israel's founding, as diverse elements of the society grapple with this dilemma. Each of these Zionisms offers its own interpretation of the problem and promise of a solution.

Mainstream Zionism
Most Israelis identify themselves as Zionists, supporters of the concept of Israel being a homeland for the Jewish people. Even so, voting behavior among Zionists is divided among the nation's three largest political parties: Kadima, Labor, and Likud. Ten smaller parties, with at least three seats in the Israeli Parliament, or Knesset, also play a role in contemporary Zionism.

At the time of Israel's founding in 1948, Labor Zionism emerged as the dominant political and economic force. It competed for attention with Socialist Zionism, the agrarian utopianism that underlay the kibbutzim movement. Both political tendencies were secular and, at times, even antagonistic to the religious component of Judaism. But the secular Zionists did create coalitions with the religious parties in order to form a functioning government. Together they even wove a founding myth of the nation in which Palestinian resentments and violence at being displaced to create the Jewish state became reframed as "pogroms" and thus nearly indistinguishable from the atrocities committed by the Nazis. Avraham Burg asserted in *The Holocaust Is Over*:

> The political manipulation that turned the Arabs into the spiritual brethren of the Nazis, or worse, conveniently allowed us to move forward in life. Restored relations with Germany and the West enabled us to receive the German reparations and compensation money. At the same time, we continued to lament our bad fortune, to express anger, to remember and never forget, by reincarnating the Nazi spirit into the Arab body.[1]

At the core of mainstream Zionist thinking was the concept of the "New Jew," a modern-day, Hebrew-speaking warrior who would never submit to oppression as Jews of the diaspora had presumably done. Embracing this concept, the center-right Likud won a dramatic electoral victory in 1977, routing the leftist Labor Party. The political culture of the Likud was more hawkish toward the Palestinians, although it was also responsible for negotiating the most important peace treaty ever signed with the Arabs, the 1979 Camp David Accords.

Prime Minister Ariel Sharon formed Kadima in the fall of 2005 after he formally left the Likud. The Israeli leader had grown frustrated at his former party's unwillingness to remove Jewish settlements from the Occupied Territories but in August 2005 had finally been able to evict settlers from Gaza and four settlement communities in the northern West Bank. Sharon perceived Kadima as a centrist party that would commit itself to the Roadmap for Peace, an initiative to resolve the Arab-Israeli conflict first articulated by President Bush in 2002. Also backed by the European Union, the United Nations, and Russia, the proposal called for the Palestinian Authority to renounce terrorism in exchange for statehood. However, renewed building of Jewish settlements on the West Bank and surprise victory in the 2006 Palestinian elections of Hamas, with whom

Israel and the United States refused to negotiate, complicated this initiative. Sharon suffered an incapacitating stroke in January 2006 and was replaced as prime minister by former Jerusalem mayor Ehud Olmert. When forced to resign on account of corruption charges, the Israeli foreign minister, Tzipi Livni, became leader of the Kadima Party.

The Neo-Zionists

In the 1970s a new interpretation of Zionism emerged as a solution to the myriad threats confronting the Jewish state. Called neo-Zionism, its adherents found a home in the Likud, the National Religious Party, and smaller parties such as Tehiva, Tzomet, and Moledet. They attacked the secular Zionism of the Labor Party for being too weak on issues of nationalism to protect the Jewish people from the threat posed by Arab nationalism. Neo-Zionists affirmed that the only solution to the problems facing Israel was "deterrence and retaliation."[2] They referred to the Occupied Territories by their biblical names—Judaea and Samaria—and publicly yearned for the day when Jews would control all of Israel.

The organizational spearhead of the movement was Gush Emunim. The organization offered young religious Jews, who had until then felt adrift and in search of their roots, a renewed purpose in life. A messianic movement awaiting the coming of the Jewish Messiah, its goal was that of *Eretz Yisrael* (Greater Israel). The group intended to accomplish its aims by establishing settlements in the Palestinian-occupied Gaza and West Bank territories, which Israel had captured during the 1967 Six-Day War.

The Israeli government encouraged Jewish migration to settlements in the Occupied Territories by offering financial benefits and incentives to Israelis who did move. The settler population had swelled to nearly 500,000 by 2005 when Sharon dismantled the settlements in Gaza.

In *The End of Days* Gershom Gorenberg remarked:

> Success and burning enthusiasm made the Gush the leading force in religious Zonism. The victory of Menachem Begin's Likud party in the 1977 election looked like one more proof that God was directing history as the Gush expected. For the first time, the expansionist right ruled Israel. Thousands of Gush Emunim settlers moved into the occupied territories, to which they referred by the Hebrew acronym

Yesha—meaning salvation. Messianists had become legitimate partners in national policy.[3]

Israeli professor Ofira Seliktar has defined neo-Zionism as an ideology in which ". . . military conflict is considered preferable to a compromise over the territories. Calls to surrender Judaea and Samaria are
often equated with inviting physical annihilation or life in compromise and submission."[4]

Armchair Zionists

Israelis have sometimes resented the fact that most American Jews have no
intention of immigrating to Israel. And yet the Americans look to that tiny
nation for spiritual sustenance and redemption and as an oasis of ethnic
homogeneity in a world gobbling up the Judaic lineage through assimila-
tion and intermarriage. For this reason, Israelis have been known to refer
to their American cousins as "armchair Zionists." But the commitment of
these diasporan men and women to the future of the Jewish state is all-
embracing. Israeli diplomat and politician Abba Eban once remarked: "For
American Jews, an enemy of Israel is someone who agrees with Israel 95
percent of the time."

In recent years the twin weapons systems wielded by "armchair Zionists" to ensure Israel's survival have been the AIPAC and the ideology of
neo-conservatism. In 2007 Professor Walt and Professor Mearsheimer issued a controversial working paper that later turned into the book entitled
The Israel Lobby and U.S. Foreign Policy. Walt and Mearsheimer described
AIPAC as a "de facto agent for a foreign government," with a "stranglehold
on Congress."[5]

Conversely, neoconservatism called for a proactive stance in foreign
policy matters and a "global democratic revolution." Two New York Jewish intellectuals, Irving Kristol, cofounder of *Encounter* magazine, and
Norman Podhoretz, editor of *Commentary* magazine, first articulated this
ideology in the 1970s. Neoconservatives pushed the utopianist notion that
democracy could be imposed on Middle Eastern countries by force and
that once accomplished, such nations would embrace the notion of making peace with Israel.

In 1996 a paper entitled "A Clean Break: A New Strategy for Securing the Realm" was sent to incoming Israeli prime minister Benjamin

Netanyahu. Its signatories, including Donald Rumsfeld, Paul Wolfowitz, Elliott Abrams, and Richard Perle, advocated regime change in Iraq and disagreed with international pressures to return the Occupied Territories to the Palestinians. They also came to hold top positions in the Bush administration and pushed forward their agenda using well-funded think tanks such as the American Enterprise Institute, the Hudson Institute, and the Washington Institute for Near East Policy (established in 1985 by the research director of the Israeli lobbying group AIPAC).

The Bush doctrine of preemptive war in furtherance of U.S. foreign policy interests emerged from this ideological stockpot and became the impetus for the Bush administration's 2003 invasion of Iraq. However, disillusionment has set in since then given the fact that the Iraq invasion became a recruitment bonanza for anti-Israel militants. At the same time, democratic elections brought Hamas to power in the Palestinian parliament in 2006, and this party's charter calls for the destruction of Israel through jihad. Columnist Juan Cole has even declared neo-conservatism was dead in Gaza. In a January 2009 piece, he asserted:

> The Gaza War of 2009 is a final and eloquent testimony to the complete failure of the neoconservative movement in United States foreign policy. For over a decade, the leading figures in this school of thought saw the violent overthrow of Saddam Hussein and the institution of a parliamentary regime in Iraq as the magic solution to all the problems in the Middle East. They envisioned, in the wake of the fall of Baghdad, the moderation of Hezbollah in Lebanon, the overthrow of the Baath Party in Syria and the Khomeinist regime in Iran, the deepening of the alliance with Turkey, the marginalization of Saudi Arabia, a new era of cheap petroleum, and a final resolution of the Israeli-Palestinian conflict on terms favorable to Israel. After eight years in which they strode the globe like colossi, they have left behind a devastated moonscape reminiscent of some post-apocalyptic B movie. As their chief enabler prepares to exit the White House, the only nation they have strengthened is Iran; the only alliance they have deepened is that between Iran and two militant Islamist entities to Israel's north and south, Hezbollah and Hamas.[6]

But far from giving up, some neoconservatives in the U.S. foreign policy establishment have turned their sights on Iran. In an August 21, 2007, article in the *Nieman Watchdog* project, Dan Froomkin wrote: "A small group of neoconservatives [are] ever-more-loudly beating the drums for military action against Iran—and getting a lot of attention."[7]

Lukewarm Zionists

In a 2005 survey conducted by the Israel Project, it was reported that only 53 percent of American Jews between the ages of 18 and 29 supported Israel compared to 67 percent of those aged sixty-five and older. The poll also found a diminishing number of Jews interested or willing to defend Israel's policies.[8] Another poll taken in 2006 by the Andrea and Charles Bronfman Philanthropies found that "only 48 percent of young Jews surveyed said that they would regard the destruction of Israel as a personal tragedy."[9]

With the December 2008 invasion of Gaza, Israel found itself facing "a strategic loss on the battlefield of public perception," according to Canadian journalist, Jeet Heer. In a *National Post* column he asserted:

> As it did in earlier wars where Israel killed large numbers of civilians, global public opinion is cooling toward the Jewish state, which runs the risk of becoming an international pariah.
>
> This shift in public opinion is most striking when we look at young Jews in North America, who are much more critical of Israel than their parents and grandparents. Given the fact that Israel has always relied heavily on support, both financial and moral, from the Diaspora, the loss of loyalty of young Jews is a dangerous trend.
>
> Evidence of the turn against Israel by large parts of the Diaspora can be seen everywhere, from protests to comedy shows. In Toronto, a group of Jewish women briefly occupied the Israeli consulate in protest against the war. In Los Angeles, young Jews wearing keffiyehs marched outside the Israeli consulate carrying signs reading "Difference Between Warsaw Ghetto & Gaza? 70 Years."[10]

Orthodox Anti-Zionists

It was to be expected that the Arab world would be vehemently anti-Zionist. After all, Zionism demanded their lands for the state of Israel. What the Israeli polity might not have anticipated were the permutations that anti-Zionism would take among Orthodox Jews, or *Haredim*. More than 40 percent of the population of Israel is now Orthodox and ultra-Orthodox Jews. A growing number of these people are anti-Zionist.

Professors Shahak and Mezvinsky have explained the opposition of the Haredim to the Zionist message:

> In a famous Talmudic passage . . . God is said to have imposed three oaths on the Jews. Two of these oaths that clearly contradict Zionist tenets are: 1. Jews should not rebel against non-Jews, and 2. as a group should not massively emigrate to Palestine before the coming of the Messiah. (The third oath. . . enjoins the Jews not to pray too strongly for the coming of the Messiah, so as not to bring him before his appointed time.)[11]

From its inception, a small Orthodox sect called Neturei Karta actively opposed the creation of Israel. Its leaders expressed the fear that the Jewish state was itself the greatest threat to world Jewry since the Holocaust. Their beliefs stemmed from an interpretation of the scriptures that saw Judaism as a religion of the spirit. The more central the Jewish state became to defining Judaism itself, their spokesmen declared, the weaker would become the spiritual and human values upon which their religion was based. A Jewish state, they also argued, would not be immune to the problems of all states, including militarism, unsavory political dealings, and financial scandals.[12]

Another Orthodox sect, Satmar—one of the largest Hasidic sects in the world—broadcast a similar message. The late Satmar rabbi and Talmudic scholar, Joel Teitelbaum, asserted that only the Messiah himself would have the divine mandate to bring Jewish communities from around the world together in a Jewish state. Thus secular attempts were doomed to failure. Far worse, according to Satmar teachings, was the prediction that since Zionism was a heresy, which conflicted with the Torah, Jews now in Israel should expect a cataclysm to befall them reflecting God's wrath. Orthodox Jews of the Satmar Hasidim and Shomer Emunim Hasidim, the Neturei Karta, and the Edah HaChareidis sects believe that the Jewish state of Israel should be dismantled.

In *A Threat from Within: A Century of Jewish Opposition to Zionism*, Professor Yakov M. Rabkin wrote: "Zionism epitomises not only the very worst of European nationalism—exclusivism that leads to genocidal violence, but the triumph of arrogance and a lust for power that run counter to the commands of the Torah."[13]

To many mainstream Zionists, the views of these groups are bizarre and incomprehensible. In a 2005 sermon Rabbi Lisa Hochberg-Miller of Ventura, California, bemoaned the fact that when the Israeli national anthem "is played in the Knesset, democratically elected ultra-Orthodox Knesset members remain seated or worse, walk out, to stand in the hallway with the Arab members of the Knesset, who also have vacated the Knesset chamber. . . ."[14]

The New Historians and Sociologists

In the mid-1980s the Israeli archives adopted a policy of declassifying official documents. Thousands of pages of government reports became available to scholars and journalists. Historians like Professor Benny Morris and Tom Segev began revising the history of the young nation in light of what they found. In the process many of Israel's most cherished founding myths were fed into the shredder. Professor Morris coined the term "New Historians" to refer to the work of revisionists like himself who repudiated the David versus Goliath myth of Israel's founding in favor of one that juxtaposed the victimization of the Palestinians alongside the successes of Zionism. The New Historians also contrasted themselves with those activist-intellectuals who had participated in Israel's founding and were thus unable to separate themselves from the events about which they wrote.[15] In fact, this younger generation of historians accused Israel's elder statesmen of sculpting a collective memory that gave existential meaning to the Zionist enterprise while suppressing that which contradicted the young state's belief in its moral right to exist.

In *A History of Modern Palestine: One Land, Two Peoples*, Professor Ilan Pappé reevaluated Zionist strategies during the British Mandate period and contradicted earlier Israeli historians by declaring that the Palestinians were intentionally expelled from their lands during Israel's 1948 War of Independence. Author Uri Milstein offered a harsh evaluation of the performance of the IDF in his *History of Israel's War of Independence*, as well as a comprehensive study of the diplomatic and military narrative surrounding Israel's 1948 War of Independence. In his book, *The Politics of Partition*, Professor Shlaim challenged much of the folklore that has sprung up around the creation of Israel. His book *The Iron Wall: Israel and the Arab World* identified a Zionist strategy of building the Jewish homeland into such a powerful military fortress, that the Arabs would finally see the futility of fighting against it. Tom Segev's book *The Seventh Million* asserted that Zionist leaders during World War II were far more preoccupied with trying to establish a homeland in Palestine than in saving Jews from the Holocaust. In *One Palestine, Complete: Jews and Arabs under the British Mandate*, Segev discussed the evolution of two incompatible nationalisms, that of the Jews and of the Palestinians. His book *1967* detailed a plan to transfer local Palestinians to Iraq, although the plan was never carried out.

These scholars held diverse views about the circumstances that led to the creation of Israel. However, where they did agree was that the "official" version of Israel's founding was mythological. While traditional accounts asserted that the Palestinians freely departed their homes for refugee camps, the New Historians disputed that. They argued among themselves, however, as to whether the displacement of the Palestinians was a conscious policy of the Israel's founders or an unplanned consequence of war.

Following in the path of these revisionist historians was a movement of social scientists, referred to as the New Sociologists. Scholars like Professor Uri Ram of Ben-Gurion University; Baruch Kimmerling, a sociology professor at Hebrew University of Jerusalem; and Yehouda Shenhav, head of Advanced Studies at the Van Leer Jerusalem Institute questioned the moral validity of the Zionist enterprise, identifying it as just another form of colonialism. Shenhav also accused the Israeli Zionist Left of being "willing to invest its all in exposing the injustices which were inflicted, and are still inflicted, on the Palestinians, but is not willing to take a stand in denouncing the racism of its parents' generation toward the Mizrahi Jews."[16]

The Israeli Post-Zionists

A new worldview began to emerge in the aftermath of the Oslo Peace Accords signed in 1994. It was framed by the reinterpretations of Israeli society contained in the works of the New Historians and Sociologists. At first these scholars were dismissed as self-hating Jews. But over time, Israeli society began to define its voice as a new cultural discourse. Post-Zionist has become the preferred name for secular intellectuals and peace activists who believe that Israel has fulfilled its initial purpose and must now evolve into a secular democracy that privileges neither Jews nor Arabs. Post-Zionist public intellectuals include Ilan Pappé, Tom Segev, and Tanya Reinhart. The post-Zionists believe that their efforts are the only way to force Jews to see and understand the true nature of Arab resentments and lay the basis for eventual peace between the two camps.

In time scholars with post-Zionist sensibilities diverged into what some scholars came to refer to as soft-core and hard-core tendencies. Scholars like Benny Morris insisted that Zionism was morally justified in creating a homeland for the Jews because of the urgency of their plight in fleeing the Holocaust. According to University of Washington professor Deborah L. Wheeler, hard-core post-Zionists "don't deny the perilous situation of Jews before 1948," but they do "view Zionism as settler colonialism that disenfranchised another community, and they refuse to view it as a moral solution to the Jewish problem."[17]

Post-Zionist modes of thinking have not been limited to academics. Avraham Burg penned an explosive article in *The London Guardian* entitled "The End of Zionism: Israel Must Shed its Illusions and Choose between Racist Oppression and Democracy." Burg began:

> The Zionist revolution has always rested on two pillars: a just path and an ethical leadership. Neither of these is operative any longer. The Israeli nation today rests on a scaffolding of corruption, and on foundations of oppression and injustice. As such, the end of the Zionist enterprise is already on our doorstep. There is a real chance that ours will be the last Zionist generation. There may yet be a Jewish state here, but it will be a different sort, strange and ugly. . . . The countdown to the end of Israeli society has begun.[18]

Later interviewed in *The New Yorker*, Burg asserted:

> People are not willing to admit it, but Israel has reached the wall. Ask your friends if they are certain their children will live here. How many will say yes? At most 50 percent. In other words, the Israeli elite has already parted with this place. And without the elite there is no nation.[19]

In 2003 Daniel Gavron, a lifelong Zionist, published *The Other Side of Despair: Jews and Arabs in the Promised Land*. He believed that Israel would pay a moral penalty for "the settlers' single-minded pursuit of Greater Israel." Gavron wrote:

> Many Israelis, and other Jews, will argue that historic justice demands a Jewish state. They will insist that, particularly after centuries of horrendous Jewish suffering culminating in the Holocaust, there should be one place on Earth where the Jews can exercise their natural right to sovereignty. They are absolutely right, but, unfortunately, given the choice between sovereignty and land, we chose land. We have manifestly preferred settlement in the whole Land of Israel to a state of Israel in part of the land. It is irrelevant that the settlers are a small minority. The rest of us have permitted them to do what they wanted.[20]

The New York Post-Zionists

In 1997 Edward Said, the late Palestinian-American scholar, publicly called for abandonment of the Oslo Accord's two-state solution in favor of a one-state vision. Said wrote:

> It has been the failing of Oslo to plan in terms of separation, a clinical partition of peoples into individual, but unequal, entities rather than to grasp that the only way of rising beyond the endless back-and-forth violence and dehumanization is to admit the universality and integrity of the other's experience, and to begin to plan a common life together.[21]

But the post-Zionist notion of Israel becoming a binational state (one nation of two peoples) only exploded onto the Jewish-American landscape in October 23, 2003, when Tony Judt, a history professor at New York University, wrote an essay entitled "Israel: The Alternative" in *The New York Review of Books*. Judt asserted:

> The situation of Israel is not desperate, but it may be close to hopeless. What sensible Israelis fear much more than Hamas or the al-Aqsa Brigade is the steady emergence of an Arab majority in "Greater Israel," and above all the erosion of the political culture and civic morale of their society.[22]

Judt then posed the question:

> . . . what if there were no place in the world today for a "Jewish state"?
> What if the one-state solution were not just increasingly likely, but
> actually a desirable outcome? It is not such a very odd thought. Most
> of the readers of this essay live in pluralist states which have long since
> become multiethnic and multicultural. . . . Western civilization today
> is a patchwork of colors and religions and languages, of Christians,
> Jews, Muslims, Arabs, Indians, and many others—as any visitor to
> London or Paris or Geneva will know. Israel itself is a multicultural
> society in all but name; yet it remains distinctive among democratic
> states in its resort to ethnoreligious criteria with which to denominate
> and rank its citizens.[23]

The response to Judt's piece was swift and ruthless. Denounced by
Zionist leaders as a self-hating Jew, Judt's name was removed by the literary editor of *The New Republic*, Leon Wieseltier, from the magazine's mast-
head. Several zealots went so far as to threaten him and his family with
bodily harm. Judt's threat to the Zionist establishment lay in his ability to
articulate another course for Israel, one in which its survival was not contingent on the survival of a state that privileged Jews at the expense of its other
citizens.

The Critics

Evidence of the growing strength of post-Zionism within Israeli society is
the number of articles and books now being published to refute it. Yoram
Hazony has become the voice of this reaction. His book *The Jewish State:
The Struggle for Israel's Soul* explores how deeply post-Zionist ideas have
come to permeate Israeli society. Hazony complains bitterly that Israeli
public figures demand the de-Judaization of the Israeli flag and national
anthem and the Ministry of Education's archaeology curriculum makes no
mention of Jews, Judaism, or the Jewish people. Even the military has been
influenced by this damnable ideology as far as Hazony is concerned. The
IDF no longer articulates its mission as one of serving as a guardian for
Jewish people. Rather it speaks of "the safeguarding of state, citizens, and
democracy." Dr. Martin Sherman, a political science professor at Tel Aviv
University, has also insisted that a post–Zionist state will erode the Jewish
population of Israel. He asserts:

After all, if Israel is not a Jewish state, there will be absolutely no motivation for, nor reason, why highly educated, highly skilled and highly trained Jews from across the developed world should aspire to make their homes here—not scientists, not doctors, not engineers not entrepreneurs, not academics.[24]

The American Jewish community has tended to attack both Orthodox anti-Zionists and secular post-Zionists as self-hating Jews, "a knife in the back of the nation," or something even worse—*kapos*. This was the name given to traitors who served as guards in the Nazi death camps in order to win favors for themselves. Steven Spielberg, once the toast of Zionist society for producing *Schindler's List*, fell into disfavor amid harsh criticisms after the release of *Munich*, a cinematic work reflecting clear post-Zionist sensibilities toward the "victimized" Palestinians.

9

The Debate

While post-Zionists have come to permeate the Israeli intelligentsia, the artistic community, and university classrooms, it is still not a popular view within the Israeli electorate. Not a single political party openly embraces the concept of creating a non-Jewish state. Neither do any of the main branches of Judaism in America, although Reform Zionism prior to the Holocaust took a strong, anti-Zionist stance. In fact, some Israelis now assert that post-Zionism ended in bloodshed and disillusionment in September 2000 with the eruption of the Second Intifada. In 2004 Dalia Shecori wrote an article for the *Haaretz* newspaper entitled "Post-Zionism Is Dead or in a Deep Freeze." In the article, she quoted Professor Pappé, who declared:

> Many of the people whom I defined as critical and courageous turned out to be chickens. Some of them even admitted that they were recanting, some just lowered their profile and nowadays it is very hard to find in Israeli academic institutions what we found there in the 1990s.[1]

In April 2004 Ami Isseroff, director of a popular Israeli blog MidEastWeb, wrote a column entitled "Post-Zionism: Requiem for an

Intellectual Fad." He asserted: "Whatever [post–Zionism] was, if it was ever more than a name, it is probably dead."[2] Professor Morris, who had a decade before being identified as one of the founders of the movement, even went so far as to renounce the very premise on which the post-Zionist movement was based—sympathy for the plight of the Palestinian refugees. He declared in a 2004 interview that "Ben-Gurion was right. . . . Without the uprooting of the Palestinians, a Jewish state would not have arisen here."[3]

But post-Zionism is not dead. What critics of the movement took for its disappearance was merely a drawback, the waters receding from the coastline as a tsunami rears up on the horizon. It is sweeping across the landscape of the Occupied Territories, drowning calls for an independent Palestinian state. Some scholars have even termed this new ideology Post-post–Zionism as a way of distinguishing the new movement from its more idealized beginnings in the Jewish intellectual community of the 1990s.

Contemplating One State

The status of Arab citizens of Israel is at the core of the new post-Zionist push to democratize Israel. Having captured the West Bank and Gaza in 1967, Israelis must grapple with prospects of a Palestinian majority in their own country. That fact has Jewish officials terrified. In November 2007 Israeli prime minister Ehud Olmert warned: "If the day comes when the two-state solution collapses, and we face a South African-style struggle for equal voting rights, then, as soon as that happens, the State of Israel is finished."[4]

But the two-state solution may have already collapsed. On the same day that Olmert's comments appeared in the Israeli press, 67 prominent Israeli and Palestinian academics and activists issued their own "One State Declaration," in which they committed themselves to "a democratic solution that will offer a just, and thus enduring, peace in a single state." It repudiated the partitioning of Israel into one Jewish state and one Palestinian state, claiming that the two-state solution:

> . . . entrenches and formalizes a policy of unequal separation on a land that has become ever more integrated territorially and economically. All the international efforts to implement a two-state solution cannot conceal the fact that a Palestinian state is not viable, and that Palestinian

and Israeli Jewish independence in separate states cannot resolve fundamental injustices, the acknowledgment and redress of which are at the core of any just solution.[5]

Since 2005, four books have come out advocating the one-state solution. Virginia Tilley, a political science professor, published *The One-State Solution: A Breakthrough for Peace in the Israeli-Palestinian Deadlock* in May 2005. While some, like Mark Satin, editor of the *Radical Middle Newsletter*, called Tilley's book "sensible and visionary," others, like British law professor John Strawson accused the author of being "light-minded" and "careless," concluding that "Israelis and Palestinians in large numbers favor a two state solution and that is what they both deserve."[6] One customer who read the book even went so far as to insist: "Tilley and others who call for Israel's replacement by a 'unitary Palestine' know full well that this would lead to a second Holocaust of Israel's five million Jews."[7]

In October 2006 Ali Abunimah came out with another controversial book, the one entitled *One Country: A Bold Proposal to End the Israeli-Palestinian Impasse*. In laying out a case for a unitary state, he said: "The point is not to deny Jews a safe haven in Palestine-Israel, but to make the necessary changes that can at least allow it to become one for the first time since Israel was founded."[8] Two months later, a group of prominent Arab-Israeli mayors called on Israel to redefine itself as a "consensual democracy for both Arabs and Jews." The report, entitled "The Future Vision of the Palestinian Arabs in Israel," proposed a form of government based on the Belgian model for French and Flemish speakers. It would involve proportional representation and power sharing in a centralized state. Not surprisingly, some Jewish Israelis responded with empathy while others expressed indignation at the mere thought of such radical change, which would ultimately negate the Jewishness of the dtate.[9]

In February 2007 writer Joel Kovel published *Overcoming Zionism: Creating a Single Democratic State in Israel/Palestine*. Kovel argued that Israel's only hope for peace was to reform itself into a new country in which Israelis and Palestinians coexist in a secular democracy. In June 2007 Dr. Ghada Karmi published *Married to Another Man: Israel's Dilemma in Palestine*.[10] The book's title was borrowed from a telegraph message sent by two Swiss rabbis in 1897 to the First Zionist Congress. They had undertaken a fact-finding mission to Palestine in order to determine whether it might be an appropriate venue for a future Jewish homeland. The two men cabled back: "The bride is beautiful but she is married to another man," making reference to the fact that their hoped-for Jewish homeland was already occupied by the Palestinians. In *Married to Another Man* Dr. Karmi declared:

> A single state that is secular and democratic for all its citizens, offers much more hope for peace than a state based on Jewish exclusivity next to a truncated and utterly unviable proposed Palestinian state under Israel's vice-like control.[11]

Questions and Answers

Israel is the only "true" democracy in the Middle East. So, isn't it already a state of all its citizens?

Professor Steven Plaut of the University of Haifa has insisted: "Israel *is* a state of all its citizens." He asserted:

> It is a democracy and all its citizens vote, enjoy free access to courts, can run for office, and enjoy freedom of speech. Of course the large majority of all its citizens happen to be Jews who happen to think that Israel has a right to exist as a state with a Jewish majority and with a Jewish character as legitimate as France being French. There is a minority of hostile disloyal Israeli Arabs who do not want Israel to exist as a state of all its citizens, but granting them their wishes is hardly the creation of a "state for all its citizens."[12]

Unfortunately, Arab citizens of Israel proper and some Jews do not see that nation as one in which Arabs and Jews are treated equally. In September 2004 a report of the Israeli Commission of Inquiry into the events precipitating the eruption of Arab violence in the Second Intifada was released. Theodor Or, a retired Israeli Supreme Court justice, wrote:

> The Arab citizens of Israel live in a reality in which they experience discrimination as Arabs. This inequality has been documented in a large number of professional surveys and studies, has been confirmed in court judgments and government resolutions, and has also found expression in reports by the state comptroller and in other official

documents. Although the Jewish majority's awareness of this discrimination is often quite low, it plays a central role in the sensibilities and
attitudes of Arab citizens. This discrimination is widely accepted, both
within the Arab sector and outside it, and by official assessments, as a
chief cause of agitation.[13]

Israel operates a social system that is "separate but unequal." It spends
40 percent less on the education of Palestinian children than it does on
Jewish children. The government provides a higher level of social services
to Jews than it does to Arabs within the society. According to a report
issued by the Legal Center for Arab Minority Rights in Israel, no fewer
than seventeen Israeli laws deprive Palestinians of basic rights, including exclusion from certain government jobs, restricted land and water rights, and
inferior educational opportunities.[14]

Isn't this "one-state proposal" just a thinly veiled ploy to destroy the Jewish state?
Harvard professor Alan Dershowitz called the one-state solution "anti-
Semitic," declaring: "Those who advocate the single state solution would
never do so with regard to India, the former Yugoslavia, or other previ-
ously united states which have now been divided on ethnic or religious
grounds."[15] Sol Stern and Fred Siegel wrote a column in the *New York Sun*
attacking the one-state solution as

> a euphemism for the destruction of the Jewish state—a trope of the
> most extreme rejectionist elements within the Palestinian movement
> and their allies in Syria and Iran. Terrorist groups such as Hamas and
> Hezbollah want to create an Islamic Republic in place of Israel.[16]

The one-state proposal is not a ploy designed to destroy the Jewish
state. It is the only option remaining that can save Israel from perpetual warfare. The Jewish state is crumbling from within, its citizens
exhausted and confused by the hostility engendered by their statehood.
The more fearful the nation becomes, the more likely that fanaticism
rather than reason could embroil it in a suicidal war with its neighbors.
Most thinkers and activists who promote the one-state solution do not
question Israel's *right* to exist as a Jewish state. Rather, as Mark Satin
has noted, they:

question the *wisdom* of its existing as a specifically Jewish state when Jewish life and culture could be equally well (and arguably more securely and benignly) preserved in that same region in a secular, democratic state that was constitutionally sensitive to the needs of all its people.[17]

Why should Jews, who have already suffered unspeakable horrors at the hands of anti-Semites, be expected to give up that which they cherish the most, their statehood?

It is because the West, unwittingly, lured the Jewish people into a trap after World War II. Europe and the United States, unwilling to make a home for survivors of the Holocaust, merely hid behind Zionist calls for a Jewish homeland in Palestine. During World War II, Western nations had refused to open their borders to Jews fleeing Nazi persecution. Given the sordid history of Western anti-Semitism and the death of six million Jews in concentration camps on account of it, the West owed Jewish survivors, at the very least, a state carved out of Germany rather than a colonial possession in the Middle East, inhabited by enraged Arabs. It is true that many religious Zionists offer biblical justification for building the Jewish homeland in Palestine. But it is also the case that the majority of Orthodox Jews opposed Zionism in the years preceding the establishment of Israel. However, once the state came into being, the Orthodox sects chose a range of approaches to its existence. Neturei Karta, the Edah HaChareidis, and the Satmar Hasidim, for instance, have continued to maintain an anti-Zionist stance. They warn that the Torah forbade Jews from having their own state until after the arrival of the Messiah, at which point it would be brought into being through the work of divine will rather than through human agency. Transgressing such a fundamental biblical law, they believe, can only lead to tragedy for the Jewish people.

Dr. George E. Bisharat, a law professor at Hastings College of the Law in San Francisco, has laid out five advantages of the one-state solution:

> First, it would transform 1.4 million Palestinian residents of Israel from a subordinated minority to full citizens. Second, it would permit genuine realization of the right of return of roughly 4 million Palestinian refugees by providing a greater geographical range for their resettlement. Third, it would enable Jewish Israelis to continue to choose to live in parts of the West Bank that are of religious and cultural

significance to them. Fourth, it would vault over two of the thorniest issues that plague the two-state solution: the drawing of borders of the new Palestinian state and the division of Jerusalem. Fifth, while it would require both peoples to surrender their deeply cherished dreams of exclusive sovereignty, this sacrifice would be reciprocal and would result in a more equitable distribution of rights overall. Finally—for now—and most importantly, because it would resolve major outstanding injustices, it would lead to durable peace in the region.[18]

Isn't this one-state idea just a trick being pushed by Libyan leader Muammar Qaddafi, Hamas, Iran, and Syria to impose a radical Islamic state on the region?

It is true that on January 21, 2009, Qaddafi, who used to call for Israeli Jews to be tossed into the sea, wrote an op-ed piece in the *New York Times* entitled "The One-State Solution." The Libyan leader declared: "A two-state solution will create an unacceptable security threat to Israel. An armed Arab state, presumably in the West Bank, would give Israel less than 10 miles of strategic depth at its narrowest point."[19] The Libyan leader's moderate tone might have represented diplomatic grandstanding as Barack Obama became president of the United States. Or maybe Qaddafi merely changed his mind regarding previous threats against Israel.

However, Iran, Syria, and Hamas are not pushing the one-state solution. In fact, moderate Palestinians, who do not want to be ruled by the radical Hamas, have shown growing interest in this one-state proposal. As for imposing a radical Islamic state in the region, it is the continuing conflict and the intolerable living conditions for Palestinians that fuel support for Hamas and the Muslim fundamentalists.

How is this one-state solution going to save Israel from a second Holocaust?

It will bring peace to the Middle East. Zionism has demonized the grievances of the Palestinians, confusing Arab rage at being ejected from their homeland with the irrational lunacy of the Nazis. Given the horrors of the Holocaust compounded by interminable wars with the Arabs, it is only natural that Israeli Jews would feel paranoid and distrustful. But it is for this reason that the United States and other outside actors must take the lead. Just as the Afrikaners in South Africa stoked fears of bloody revenge, Zionists have Israelis worried that all they can expect of Palestinians will be irrational violence and the extermination of the Jews. It is not easy to maintain the capacity to trust given what Jews have endured throughout history. But it is a necessary component for all nations that attain peace. Those Israelis who are unable to overcome their visceral fear and hatred of Arabs should be given the opportunity to leave the Middle East and re-settle in the West, regardless of whether they can trace their ancestry to pre-Holocaust Europe.

How can this one-state solution ever happen when Jews see it as a threat to their security and there is, as a consequence, no political constituency in Israel pushing for it?

It will either have to be sold to Israelis by concerned allies, or the security situation will continue to deteriorate until Israelis see that they have no choice if their homeland is to survive. More to the point, if the Israelis could forgive Germany for the Holocaust, which, given the cordial relations the two nations enjoy, they have, then they can forgive the Arabs for fighting to regain their homeland.

Why should Israel be singled out for one-state statehood when the world has accepted the successful partitioning of Ireland, India, and the former Yugoslavia?

Even Israeli leftists like Uri Avnery oppose the notion of a single, bi-national state, declaring:

> In the entire world there is no example of two different nations decid-ing of their own free will to live together in one state. There is no example—except Switzerland—of a bi-national or multi-national state really functioning. (And the example of Switzerland, which has grown for centuries in a unique process, is the proverbial exception that proves the rule.)[20]

Hillel Halkin, in an article entitled "If Israel Ceased to Exist," asserts:

> A bi-national [one-state] Israel/Palestine would in all likelihood quickly degenerate into another Lebanon, with a demoralized and contracting population of Israeli Jews, steadily depleted by emigration, taking the place of Lebanese Christians.[21]

In Ireland, India, and the former Yugoslavia, it was possible to physically separate the populations into separate territories. In the case of the so-called Palestinian state, Israel controls its borders and its economic viability. Not surprisingl observers do not so much see a Palestinian state as a bunch of politically and economically nonviable South African Bantustans.

Isn't this one-state idea a formula for endless ethnic strife? After all, the Palestinians cannot even get their own act together with fighting between Fatah and Hamas.

A one-state solution would result in combining the IDF and police with the various Palestinian security organizations and militias. This shared responsibility for security matters would be far more effective in controlling violence than matters now stands with Palestinians and Israelis attacking each other and the Palestinian factions fighting among themselves. In the early years of implementing the one-state solution, the nation might even demand that NATO troops ensure a smooth integration of all forces. Sacrifices would be required of all sides. But the end result would be a durable peace between Arabs and Israelis.

Who, other than Arabs and Muslims, is pushing this one-state plan?

One-state proponents include Israeli intellectuals like Professor Pappé and Meron Benvenisti, a political scientist and former deputy mayor of Jerusalem. He states: "Israelis and Palestinians are sinking together into the mud of 'one state.' We need a model that fits this reality. . . . The question is no longer whether it will be bi-national, but which model to choose."[22] Israeli journalists Haim Hanegbi and Daniel Gavron and Israeli-American anthropologist Jeff Halper also advocate a one-state solution. American scholars and writers like Virginia Tilley; Mark LeVine, a professor of Middle East history at the University of California–Irvine; Joel Kovel; and Tony Judt press for a binational/one-state solution. Orthodox Jews of the Satmar Hasidim and Shomer Emunim Hasidim, the Neturei Karta, and the Edah HaChareidis sects believe that the Jewish state of Israel should be dismantled before it is wiped out by God's will.

Won't a two-state solution allow the Palestinians to strengthen their sense of national identity and enrich their cultural lives just as it has done for the Jewish state?

Israel has humiliated Palestinian leaders who pushed for a two-state solution by colonizing the West Bank. Jewish settlers there and in East Jerusalem approach 500,000. Israeli land claims now cover close to half of the West Bank, and expansion continues apace. Any Palestinian state would have its borders, airspace, and water rights controlled by Israel. This two-state approach would also consign the 1.4 million Palestinians who live in Israel proper to a permanent subordinate status, given the fact that they are not Jews.

There is already a world consensus, and all diplomatic efforts center around the creation of a separate Palestinian state. Why not go with the momentum?

There is no momentum. Fifteen years of diplomacy based on the two-state plan, initiated by the Oslo Accords of 1993, have failed. The two-state solution remains the declared goal of Israeli and Palestinian leaders, but in private even some Arab leaders are discussing the one-state proposal. In a 2008 interview Kadura Fares, a member of Fatah's revolutionary council, said that the emergence of one-state proposals is "a sign that the current strategy has been exhausted and it's time to rethink all our goals."[23]

A Hebron-based journalist, Khaled Amayreh, observed:

> Support for the one-state idea is more widespread among ordinary Palestinians than among intellectuals because ordinary people believe what they see, and what they see is that Israel and the West Bank are inextricably intertwined, even despite the gigantic annexation wall.[24]

Since nowhere in the Middle East are the values of democracy and equality practiced, where is the role model to come from that will protect Jewish interests in a state that they do not control?

Professor Tilley believes the South African transition could assuage Israeli fears. She says:

> Jewish fears of annihilation at the hands of native (Arab) hordes strongly recall Afrikaner fears and prejudices about Africans. Afrikaners also believed blacks incapable of democracy, and intransigently vengeful and hostile toward whites, echoing Zionist claims that Arabs are capable only of dictatorship. South Africa's transition may therefore offer invaluable insights toward softening Jewish fears and beliefs. Again,

such willingness clearly also requires external pressure: the international boycott and sanctions campaign against South Africa combined with internal strikes, selective sabotage and moral opprobrium to bring the South African white community to face the necessity of abandoning apartheid. But a range of conciliatory gestures also allowed whites to imagine that apartheid could be dismantled without ruin and mayhem to themselves: for example, formal ANC statements toward a "rainbow nation," secret negotiations in Europe and international guarantees.[25]

Israel is not apartheid South Africa. Why should the latter be used as a model for Israel?

Benjamin Pogrund, a former antiapartheid activist, insists the two cases are not the same. He says:

> The Israeli situation can perhaps be better likened to the United States: blacks enjoyed rights under the Constitution but the rights were not enforced for decades; it took the Supreme Court's historic judgement in Brown vs Board of Education in 1954 to begin the process of applying the law. The difference between the current Israeli situation and apartheid South Africa is emphasised at a very human level: Jewish and Arab babies are born in the same delivery room, with the same facilities, attended by the same doctors and nurses, with the mothers recovering in adjoining beds in a ward.[26]

Israel is not a twin of South Africa under apartheid. All nations bring unique characteristics to their being. But the collapsing two-state solution is transforming the hoped-for Palestinian state into the hated South African Bantustans. Professor Pappé calls the South African model "a good subject matter for a comparative study—not as an object for a hallow emulation." The Israeli professor says:

> It inspires those concerned with the Palestinian cause in two crucial directions: it offers a new orientation for a future solution instead of the two states' formula that failed—by introducing the one democratic state—and it invigorates new thinking of how the Israeli occupation can be defeated—through Boycott, Divestment and Sanctions (the BDS option).[27]

Doesn't Israel have enough problems? Why should its continued existence be tied to "a far-fetched utopian fantasy"?

Why, indeed, would Israelis go along with a one-state solution? It is because if they don't then they will lose something far more precious even than their Jewish statehood. And that is their children, slaughtered in ever more violent wars, until Israel itself becomes the ultimate death camp.

The "escapist fantasy" is not the one-state solution, but rather the effort to partition Israel into sovereign nations. Ali Abunimah calls the partition scheme "a delusional deviation." He explains:

> I want to be clear that my belief that the two-state solution is unachievable derives not from an analysis that the status quo and occupation is irreversible, since anything built by humans can be dismantled by them, but that the political dynamic that has created the present situation is irreversible within the current framework.[28]

How will a one-state solution come about if there is no political constituency in Israel pushing for it?

Uri Avnery asserts that "99.9% of Jewish Israelis want the State of Israel to exist as a state with a robust Jewish majority, whatever its borders."[29]

Ali Abunimah, a one-state advocate, acknowledges:

> any serious argument for an Israeli-Palestinian democracy in a single state must confront the reality that, at present, Israeli Jews overall are deeply hostile to the idea, viewing it as an invitation to commit suicide. . . . as Israelis come to understand that unilateral solutions based on force provide no remedies to their dilemma, there might be a greater openness to the alternatives that do exist.[30]

Professor Pappé advocates applying political pressure from the outside. He explains:

> A successful boycott campaign will not change this position in a day, but will send a clear message to this public that these positions are racist and unacceptable in the 21st century. Without the cultural and economical oxygen lines the West provides to Israel, it would be

difficult for the silent majority there to continue and believe that it is possible both to be a racist and a legitimate state in the eyes of the world.[31]

Mark Satin is even more specific. He has laid out a strategy "to convince the residents of Israel-Palestine to move in the one-state direction. . . ." It offers a ten-pronged approach:

1. Develop a vision of common citizenship.
2. Develop a vision of the worldly future.
3. Initiate public discussions of the one-state solution.
4. Reassure Israeli Jews of their security and rights.
5. Organize a Truth and Reconciliation Commission.
6. Engage in civil disobedience.
7. Form a political party calling for the one-state solution.
8. Have the human rights community apply pressure.
9. Have the United States apply pressure.
10. Have both diaspora peoples apply pressure.[32]

What will Israel's future look like if it does not embrace one-state, two people? The answer is that it will have no future.

10

The Way Ahead

The issue of Israel's future is far more than just an intellectual debate. Murderous Middle Eastern neighbors besiege the tiny Jewish state. It was established in a climate of Western anti-Semitism, so endemic and treacherous that Europe and America's seeming embrace of Zionism proved to be little more than a smokescreen for ejecting Holocaust survivors from their European roots. While Hitler solved his so-called Jewish Problem with death camps, the Allies addressed theirs by shipping Holocaust survivors to Palestine. The one exception was Great Britain, which unsuccessfully attempted to block Jewish immigration to its Mandate in the Middle East in order to placate its Arab colonies. But London refused to settle more than a smattering of Holocaust survivors in its nation. In 1939 British-Canadian novelist and painter, Wyndham Lewis, published *The Jews, Are They Human?* This satirical book attacked anti-Semitism while reminding readers of its loathsome presence. He noted: "I have friends, who detest Jews, just as some people abominate cats. They cannot sit in a room with a Jew. The dark mongoloid eye, the curled semitic lip, arouses their worst passions."[1]

Israel did in time evolve into a Jewish state. But, rather than becoming a safe haven for long-persecuted Jews as early Zionists had dreamed of, the nation morphed into what is arguably the most dangerous place on earth for the descendants of the ancient Hebrews. In fact, shared hatred of Israel has brought about a unity of purpose among otherwise fractious Sunni and Shiite communities, a goal that alluded the Islamic world for more than 1,300 years.

The root cause of the nightmare Israel now faces is not Arab nationalism. It is centuries of European anti-Semitism, which culminated in the slaughter of six million innocent Jewish civilians. Support for Zionism after the Holocaust became an ideological excuse that the West skillfully manipulated for its own benefit. Unwilling or unable for social and economic reasons to allow distraught Jewish survivors into the Western Powers' own countries, they shoved them into a rabidly anti-European Middle East.

In order to become the homeland that Jews have always yearned for, a Middle East–based haven for their Jewish identity and a place of spiritual renewal and peace rather than a military fortress, Israel will have to give up the one thing it treasures most—its Jewish statehood. Israel must evolve into a secular democracy, respecting its Arab-Jewish culture as much as or perhaps even more than its European one and become a *medinat kol ezrachehah* (a state of all its citizens). If not, it will shuffle along in the world of the undead, fighting increasingly more destructive wars until it collapses in on itself or engulfs the oil-producing Middle East in a nuclear holocaust.

Why would Israel and its American Zionist supporters go along with any one-state proposal? It is because if they don't, they will lose three things even more precious than a Jewish state: their children, their soul, and their future.

Israel, the Death Camp

The United States must find the political courage to seize the initiative. It can no longer wait on Israel to act because the Jewish state is caught in a trap whose latches cannot be sprung from the inside. Given the depth of trauma suffered by the Jewish people on account of the history of anti-Semitism, their capacity to relate to their aggrieved Arab neighbors is all too often contorted by flashbacks to the Holocaust. Avraham Burg has argued:

> We have pulled the Shoah out of its historic context and turned it into
> a plea and a generator for every deed. All is compared to the Shoah,

dwarfed by the Shoah, and therefore all is allowed—be it fences, sieges, crowns, curfews, food and water deprivation, or unexplained illnesses. All is permitted because we have been through the Shoah and you will not tell us how to behave. Everything seems dangerous to us, and our normal development as a new people, society and state is arrested. . . . Instead of developing an alternative to the Holocaustic soul, we are bogged down in it and fail to reach the riverbank of optimism that is necessary for our rescue and survival.[2]

Burg added:

I believe wholeheartedly that if we do not establish modern Israeli identity on foundations of optimism, faith in humans and full trust in the family of nations, we have no chance of existing and surviving in the long run—not as a society in a state, not as a state in the world, and not as a nation in the future.[3]

In regard to U.S. policy, Professor Pappé once remarked: "Putting pressure on Israel is a small price to pay for the sake of global peace, regional stability and reconciliation in Palestine."[4] After all, as Professors Mearsheimer and Walt have observed:

Some aspects of Israeli democracy are at odds with core American values. Unlike the US, where people are supposed to enjoy equal rights irrespective of race, religion or ethnicity, Israel was explicitly founded as a Jewish state and citizenship is based on the principle of blood kinship.[5]

And yet the Jewish state finds itself in a special dilemma because in many ways, the United States has become Israel's cultural role model. While the political audience for a binational state (one nation/two people) remains small, Israeli society may be moving, slowly but inexorably, in that direction. Tom Segev cites several examples of cautious movements toward a truly pluralist Israel—one where a one-state solution might be a possibility. He describes the controversy in 2000 when the minister of education announced that poems by Mahmoud Darwish, an exiled Israeli Arab who became a leader of the PLO, would become accepted curriculum in Israeli schools. In another case, an Israeli Arab family that decided to move to a Jewish settlement won its case before the Israeli Supreme Court. American court cases, such as the 1954 landmark school desegregation case, *Brown v. Board of Education*, were cited as part of the moral precedent.[6]

False Friends

Successive U.S. administrations deferred to AIPAC and neoconservatives in determining their policy on Israel. But for America to disempower itself strategically in the face of a possible nuclear holocaust in the oil-producing Middle East is lunacy. The West also has a moral obligation, not to the "Jewish State of Israel," but rather to the ultimate safety of the Jewish people. But why focus on the grave injustices done to Jews and not, for instance, on the injustices done to the survivors of the rape of Nanking or the Armenian genocide? The answer is two-fold. Western anti-Semitism culminating in the Holocaust created the World War II Jewish refugee problem. And Israel's only true allies are the United States and other nations of the West. However, as Israeli lawyer Daniel Seidemann once said: "[President Bush] is neither friend nor supporter of the Jewish state— because friends don't let friends drive drunk. And that is precisely what this administration is doing."[7]

Christian fundamentalists, waiting for their opportunity to convert Jews at some stage of the apocalypse, and members of Congress, cowed by AIPAC, are not true friends of the Jewish people. Denying what lays ahead is not being a trustworthy friend to anyone. Jay Bookman of the *Atlanta Journal Constitution* declared:

> The missiles acquired by its Arab enemies get longer in range and heavier in payload with every passing year. The Palestinians are producing many more babies than the Jews, threatening to change geography by demography, and international support for Israel, particularly outside the United States, is waning. According to our own analysts in the CIA and elsewhere, America's power and influence will decline in the years to come, at least in relative terms, and so will its ability to protect Israel. Somehow, Israel has to break that cycle. Somehow, it has to stop sacrificing its long-term survival hopes for short-term returns. But it will not do so without outside pressure, and that help can come from only one place—the United States.[8]

Atonement

If the nations of the West have truly healed of their anti-Semitic past, then they must prove it. They must do what they refused to do after World War II—stop hiding behind Zionism and assume greater initiative for building bridges with Israeli Jews and Arabs. First and foremost, they must confront the lingering anti-Semitism in their midst. Were the situation in the Jewish state to deteriorate beyond repair, which Western country would offer land and succor to fleeing Israelis? Have attitudes in Europe and the United States changed all that radically since the World War II lockout of Jewish refugees? However unspeakable the crimes of the Holocaust, why should Germany be the only Western nation engaged in soul-searching, when Hitler concocted his Final Solution on the belief that he was doing Europe a favor by solving its so-called Jewish Problem. And why should the Middle East, just recently emerging from European colonialism, bear the full brunt of this tragic episode in history?

A profound sense of alienation and isolation has pushed Israeli Jews to the edge of a precipice. It is those feelings of peril and utter aloneness that feed the paranoia driving Israeli society to contemplate preemptive nuclear war with Iran while battling Palestinians in the Occupied Territories. In the 2009 elections right wing Israeli politician Avigdor Lieberman stoked such fears in advocating that the citizenship of Arab Israelis be revoked on the basis of disloyalty to the Jewish state and transferred to the Palestinian Authority in the Occupied Territories.

A Spiritual Center

Some early Zionists like Asher Zvi Ginsberg saw the Jewish community in Palestine serving as a spiritual center nourishing global Judaism rather than as a sovereign state. Ginsberg taught that:

> Judaism had contributed some great and unique ideas to the world, of which the most important was that complete justice should be everywhere, among all men, and that Jews must try to set an example to all men by living a just life and building a good society themselves. In Eretz Israel Jews who were proud of this ideal would establish a society based on honesty and justice. In such a society new life would be given to Judaism. Jewish history and culture would be studied, and teachers would go out from Israel to all areas where Jews lived.

In this sense, Eretz Israel would be a spiritual center of a renewed Jewish life, and would breathe this life into all the communities of the Exile.[9]

Avraham Burg believes that it is not too late to:

redefine the relationship between the world and the Jews. We can turn the word *Jew* into a concept that is much wider than mere nationality, religion, genetics and traditions. . . . Wherever a crime against a people, helpless innocents, humanity, and humanism is committed—we will be there in any possible way, in protest, action, assistance, and even in defense and rescue.[10]

In 1999 Thomas Cahill wrote *The Gifts of the Jews: How a Tribe of Desert Nomads Changed the Way Everyone Things and Feels.* He argued that the Jewish Bible changed history by injecting a linear, forward movement to the human chronicle to replace the cyclical one that had dominated all major relations up to that time. In the latter, events and people were not unique, but rather spokes in the same great wheel, recycling themselves and thus incapable of influencing or changing the future. Cahill identifies a Jewish origin to some of the most dynamic words in the English language, such as "vocation, personal destiny, and justice." In rejecting a cyclic way of life, the Hebrew people opened their lives to the possibility of a future that would be different from the past.[11]

The Veil of Zionism

Lauding the contributions of the Jewish people might be dangerous and even counterproductive, given the fact that murderous envy on the part of European gentiles fueled Western anti-Semitism in the past. It may also not be easy because Europe and the United States have shoved their lingering anti-Semitism under Zionism's skirts for the past sixty years. In many ways, the West has never had to confront its incipient anti-Semitism because Nazi Germany made itself into such an appropriate target for demonization. Daniel Goldhagen's 1997 book, *Hitler's Willing Executioners: Ordinary Germans and the Holocaust,* encouraged that attitude. He wrote about ordinary Germans hunting down and torturing Jews and then posing cheerfully for snapshots with their victims.

While Americans hid their anti-Semitism behind the horrors of German Nazism, Avraham Burg has pointed out in *The Holocaust Is Over* that Israel may have reached too "hasty a reconciliation" with Germany after World War II. He declared:

> We will never forgive the Arabs for they are allegedly just like the Nazis, worse than the Germans. We have displaced our anger and revenge from one people to another, from an old foe to a new adversary, and so we allow ourselves to live comfortably with the heirs of the German enemy—representing convenience, wealth and high quality, while treating the Palestinians as whipping boys to release our aggression, anger and hysteria, of which we have plenty.[12]

Envisioning One State

One of the most exciting arenas of discussion involving Israel is the myriad of possibilities for how a future union of Israel and Palestine might come into being. The term "one-state solution" encompasses a range of democratic structures: federal, confederal, binational, unitary decentralized, consociational, or multi-confessional. In 2003 in the Israeli daily *Haaretz*, Meron Benvenisti suggested a system "that recognizes collective ethnic-national rights and maintains power sharing on the national-central level, with defined political rights for the minority and sometimes territorial-cantonal divisions."[13]

In 2005 the Palestinian Academic Society for the Study of International Affairs (PASSIA) published *Palestinian-Israeli Impasse: Exploring Alternative Solutions to the Palestine-Israel Conflict*. This compilation of papers presented the ideas of sixteen Jewish and Arab scholars whose approaches ranged from further attempts to jumpstart the two-state solution to papers supporting a one-state solution that would offer equal citizenship and rights while allowing the separate cultures to maintain their distinctiveness.[14]

Dr. Gary Sussman, director of research at Tel Aviv University, also pushes the concept of a binational state:

> offering power-sharing to two separate peoples with distinct collective identities within one polity. . . . The [other] alternative proposes a single democratic polity, where there is no ethnic or national distinction between citizens.[15]

Jeff Halper believes "the most practical solution seems to be a unitary democratic state offering equal citizenship for all."[16]

However, Ali Abunimah prefers the Belgian model. He says:

> About 60 percent of Belgium's population lives in the Flemish region, while the once politically dominant Walloons comprise about a third [the parallel with Arabs and Jews in a future One State is obvious - ed.]. At the federal level, Belgium has a parliamentary system with universal suffrage. . . . It has long been a convention, however, that the federal government should have an equal number of Dutch-speaking and Flemish-speaking ministers who take decisions by consensus, and it became a constitutional requirement in the early 1990s. Other "alarm bell" procedures in the Belgian constitution include a mechanism to hold up decisions opposed by three-quarters of the people in either community. . . .[17]

Professor Rabkin sees Switzerland as offering the most appropriate model for the future union of Israel and Palestine. He says the new state "could consist of cantons sovereign in matters of culture, education, worship, internal security, and local law."[18] Another advantage of this governing structure, Professor Rabkin adds, is that it "would also enable Orthodox Jews and secular Hebrews, whose relationship is also profoundly acrimonious, to live their lives according to their customs and beliefs, without the irritating interventions of the state."[19] Professor LeVine offers a model in which "the country would be split into two administrative 'cantons' that would follow the current division of the territory."[20] Professor LeVine adds: "This is the arrangement in Switzerland, where Italian, French, and German enclaves exist within the territory of a canton whose majority is of one of the other two language groups."

In 2004 Howard Cort shepherded a resolution through the United Nations Association biennial meeting calling for a compilation of alternatives for an Israeli-Palestinian peace settlement. The report he presented at the meeting was entitled "Alternative Approaches to Palestinian-Israeli Coexistence."[21] Cort presented several proposals gathered from intellectuals and activists, including a "one unitary state" proposal, in which majority rule and a constitution guaranteeing equality would prevail;

"a unitary decentralized" structure, where political power was transferred to regional or locally elected governments and a "consociational state." This last option is seen in countries suffering from major internal divisions along ethnic, religious, or linguistic lines, such as Belgium and Switzerland.

Under the federation category, Cort looked at proposals for establishing a government of partially self-governing states united under a centralized or federal government, as in the United States. He included former deputy mayor Benevisti's proposal for:

> a federal structure that will include all of historic western Palestine. Different ethnic cantons will exist under that structure. . . . They will have their own autonomy, which will express their collective rights. And it's clear, on the other side, that the settlers will have a canton. The executive of the federal government will strike some sort of balance between the two national groups.[22]

Cort's third category was that of the binational state, in which:

> Jews and Palestinians would coexist as separate communities in a federal arrangement. Each people would run its own affairs autonomously and be guaranteed the legal right to use its own language, religion and traditions. Both would participate in government in a single parliament, which would be concerned with matters of supra-communal importance, defense, resources, the economy, and so on. Such a state could be modeled on the cantonal structure of Switzerland or the bi-national arrangement of Belgium. In the Palestine/Israel case, the cantonal structure would be based on the present demographic pattern of the country where densely populated areas like the Galilee would become Arab cantons, and Jewish ones like Tel Aviv would be Jewish cantons, and so on.[23]

Never Again

In the end, Israel's future will not be decided solely by the Jewish citizens of that nation and their supporters in the Diaspora. This is as it should be, since the Jewish State was not created by Zionists alone. The emergence of the modern state of Israel was a global event, representing a confluence of historical circumstances involving the traumatized survivors of the Holocaust, Western guilt at failing to confront its own anti-Semitism, United Nations votes, and warfare. But perhaps most significant of all was the West's own blinding ignorance of both the demography of the Middle East and the toxicity of the wounds suffered by the Arabs on account of their European colonial past.

It would be premature to lay out in detail the form a binational state would take. This is because the process of debating and negotiating is a creative rather than linear one. But the first, and possibly the most difficult, step in the process will be acknowledging that the time has come to set aside the exhausting diplomatic fiction that twenty-first-century Palestinians and Jews will eventually live in separate but equal states. This is as unworkable in Israel as it was in the southern United States. As to what the new Middle Eastern state might be called, let the citizens decide. A federal system in which ethnic boundaries are defined in terms of territorial division might work. But it may prove more efficient for the nation to think in terms of protecting ethnic rights rather than geographic ones. In this way, various populations of the state would be protected by their constitutionally enshrined civil rights, rather than mere location-defined ones. The role of the international community and the moral leadership of the United States will be crucial in establishing constitutional guarantees for all groups and constituting an international force to oversee the fragile transition period.

Israel should mean more to the world than the fact, however important, that it is the guardian of the most sacred heritage of Jews, Christians, and Muslims. It should mean more to the diplomatic community than its current perception as an incurable migraine of rival nationalisms, religious, and ethnic hatreds. A piece of Israel should exist in the hearts and minds of all thoughtful men and women. It should be the voice that shouts "never again" not only for Jews, but for all who face injustice. This is the *real* Israel, the one now struggling to be born.

Appendix A

The One-State Declaration

Editor's Note: The following statement was issued by participants in the July 2007 Madrid meeting on a one-state solution and the November 2007 London Conference.

For decades, efforts to bring about a two-state solution in historic Palestine have failed to provide justice and peace for the Palestinian and Israeli Jewish peoples, or to offer a genuine process leading towards them.

The two-state solution ignores the physical and political realities on the ground, and presumes a false parity in power and moral claims between a colonized and occupied people on the one hand and a colonizing state and military occupier on the other. It is predicated on the unjust premise that peace can be achieved by granting limited national rights to Palestinians living in the areas occupied in 1967, while denying the rights of Palestinians inside the 1948 borders and in the Diaspora. Thus, the two-state solution condemns Palestinian citizens of Israel to permanent second-class status within their homeland, in a racist state that denies their rights by enacting laws that privilege Jews constitutionally, legally, politically, socially and culturally. Moreover, the two-state solution denies Palestinian

---

Source: Reprinted by permission from the *Electronic Intifada.*

refugees their internationally recognized right of return.

The two-state solution entrenches and formalizes a policy of unequal separation on a land that has become ever more integrated territorially and economically. All the international efforts to implement a two-state solution cannot conceal the fact that a Palestinian state is not viable, and that Palestinian and Israeli Jewish independence in separate states cannot resolve fundamental injustices, the acknowledgment and redress of which are at the core of any just solution.

In light of these stark realities, we affirm our commitment to a democratic solution that will offer a just, and thus enduring, peace in a single state based on the following principles:

- The historic land of Palestine belongs to all who live in it and to those who were expelled or exiled from it since 1948, regardless of religion, ethnicity, national origin or current citizenship status;
- Any system of government must be founded on the principle of equality in civil, political, social and cultural rights for all citizens. Power must be exercised with rigorous impartiality on behalf of all people in the diversity of their identities;
- There must be just redress for the devastating effects of decades of Zionist colonization in the pre- and post-state period, including the abrogation of all laws, and ending all policies, practices and systems of military and civil control that oppress and discriminate on the basis of ethnicity, religion or national origin;
- The recognition of the diverse character of the society, encompassing distinct religious, linguistic and cultural traditions, and national experiences;
- The creation of a non-sectarian state that does not privilege the rights of one ethnic or religious group over another and that respects the separation of state from all organized religion;
- The implementation of the Right of Return for Palestinian refugees in accordance with UN Resolution 194 is a fundamental requirement for justice, and a benchmark of

the respect for equality;

- The creation of a transparent and nondiscriminatory immigration policy;
- The recognition of the historic connections between the diverse communities inside the new, democratic state and their respective fellow communities outside;
- In articulating the specific contours of such a solution, those who have been historically excluded from decision-making—especially the Palestinian Diaspora and its refugees, and Palestinians inside Israel—must play a central role;
- The establishment of legal and institutional frameworks for justice and reconciliation.

The struggle for justice and liberation must be accompanied by a clear, compelling and moral vision of the destination—a solution in which all people who share a belief in equality can see a future for themselves and others. We call for the widest possible discussion, research and action to advance a unitary, democratic solution and bring it to fruition.

Madrid and London, November 29, 2007

Authored By:
Ali Abunimah, Chicago
Naseer Aruri, North Dartmouth, Massachusetts
Omar Barghouti, Jerusalem
Oren Ben-Dor, London
George Bisharat, San Francisco
Haim Bresheeth, London
Jonathan Cook, Nazareth
Ghazi Falah, Akron, Ohio
Leila Farsakh, Boston
Islah Jad, Ramallah
Joseph Massad, New York
Ilan Pappé, Totnes, UK
Carlos Prieto del Campo, Madrid
Nadim Rouhana, Haifa

Endorsed By:
Nahla Abdo, Ottawa
Rabab Abdul Hadi, San Francisco
Suleiman Abu-Sharkh, Southampton, UK
Tariq Ali, London
Samir Amin, Dakar
Gabriel Ash, Geneva, Switzerland
Mona Baker, Manchester, UK
James Bowen, Cork, Ireland
Daniel Boyarin, Berkeley
Lenni Brenner, New York City
Eitan Bronstein, Tel Aviv
Michael Chanan, London
Lawrence Davidson, West Chester, Pennsylvania

Uri Davis, Sakhnin
Endorsed By (*continued*):
Raymond Deane, Dublin
Angelo D'Orsi, Turin
Haidar Eid, Gaza
Samera Esmeir, Berkeley
Claudine Faehndrich, Neuchatel, Switzerland
Arjan El Fassed, Utrecht
As'ad Ghanem, Haifa
Jess Ghannam, San Francisco
Ramon Grosfoguel, Berkeley
Laila al-Haddad, Gaza
Haifa Hammami, London
Alan Hart, Canterbury
Jamil Hilal, Ramallah
Isabelle Humphries, Cambridge, UK
Salma Jayyusi, Boston
Claudia Karas, Frankfurt
Ghada Karmi, London
Hazem Kawasmi, Ramallah

Joel Kovel, New York City
Ronit Lentin, Dublin, Ireland
Malcolm Levitt, Southampton, UK
Yosefa Loshitzky, London
Saree Makdisi, Los Angeles
Nur Masalha, London
Ugo Mattei, Turin
Sabine Matthes, Munich
Walter Mignolo, Raleigh-Durham
Yonat Nitzan-Green, Winchester, UK
Gian Paolo Calchi Novati, Pavia, Italy
Kathleen O'Connell, Belfast
Rajaa Zoa'bi O'mari, Haifa
One Democratic State Group, Gaza
Gabriel Piterberg, Los Angeles
Claudia Prestel, Leicester
Mazin Qumsiyeh, New Haven
Michael Rosen, London
Emir Sader, Buenos Aires/Rio de Janeiro
Guenter Schenk, Strasbourg
Jules Townshend, Manchester, UK
Danilo Zolo, Florence

Each individual has authored/endorsed this statement in a personal capacity.[1]

Appendix B

Palestine/Israel: One State for All Its Citizens

Ali Abuminah

Peace in Palestine through territorial partition is a doomed fantasy and the time has come to discard it. While it may once have worked on paper, in practice the Israeli state has succeeded, through the relentless colonization of the Occupied Territories and lately its grotesque separation barrier, in its long-standing goal of rendering any workable partition impossible.

While Israel was conceived as a state for Jews, Edward Said explained in 1999, the "effort to separate (Israelis and Palestinians) has occurred simultaneously and paradoxically with the effort to take more and more land, which has in turn meant that Israel has acquired more and more Palestinians." The result is that Israel can in the long run only remain a "Jewish state" through apartheid or, as some Israeli Cabinet ministers demand, ethnic cleansing.

Armed Palestinian resistance has rendered the colonization effort extremely costly to Israel, but has been unable to stop or reverse it. The "road map" was the final test of whether a two-state solution could be realized through peaceful means. The refusal of the United States to exert any pressure

Source: Reprinted by permission from the *Electronic Intifada*.

on Israel, despite an unprecedented 51-day cease-fire by all Palestinian factions, leaves no doubt that a U.S. administration, no matter how determined its rhetoric, cannot in good faith work toward such a solution. There is no other coalition of countries that is ready, willing and able to act as a counterweight to the United States.

Recognizing years ago the implications of the intertwined population and complex geography that Israeli colonization has created, Said wrote that "the question is not how to devise means for persisting in trying to separate," Israelis and Palestinians, "but to see whether it is possible for them to live together as fairly and peacefully as possible." Said believed that the way to achieve this is in a single state.

While Said's logic and vision were irresistible, the strongest counterargument was the pragmatic one: that something like peace could be most quickly achieved through ending the occupation and establishing a state for Palestinians in East Jerusalem, the West Bank and Gaza. Moreover, an international consensus and framework of international law contemplating this outcome had been painstakingly built over three decades. To discard it, many Palestinians feared, would have been to take a leap into the unknown.

But it is inescapable now that what already exists is in effect one state: Israel, in which half the population—the Palestinians—have second-class rights or no rights at all, not even citizenship.

The insistence on partition, not on one state, is increasingly a delusional deviation from this reality. I want to be clear that my belief that the two-state solution is unachievable derives not from an analysis that the status quo of settlement and occupation is irreversible, since anything built by humans can conceivably be dismantled by them, but that the political dynamic that has created the present situation is irreversible within the current framework.

The only way to rob the Israeli colonization project of its raison d'etre is not to continue to throw ourselves into the path of a superior force, or to continue to plead with the United States, but to render the motive of territorial conquest irrelevant. In one state, all people will be able to live wherever they want, provided they obtain their homes legally on the same basis as everyone else, not through force and land theft. In other words, we have to break the link between sovereignty, ethnicity and geography within Palestine.

It is the moment, therefore, for us to declare the era of partition over and commit to a moral, just and realizable vision in which Israelis and Palestinians build a future as partners in a single state which guarantees freedom, equality and cultural self-determination to all its citizens. Refusing to make this choice now means effectively agreeing to the endless bloodshed and extremism offered by Israel's political-military establishment and Hamas.

The path to one state contains obstacles, the greatest being Jewish Israelis' desire to maintain the power and privileges they enjoy today. But whatever resources they possess, ideological opponents of one state will suffer from an insurmountable weakness: They will be arguing against the most basic and deep-rooted principles of democracy—"one person, one vote" and equality before the law.

It will take enormous efforts to convince a majority of Israelis that the security and legitimacy they will never achieve through conquest and repression can be achieved by merging their political future with that of the Palestinians. I am convinced, however, that for most Israelis, resistance to this concept will not stem from an ideological commitment to a status quo in which they are privileged and others oppressed, but will arise from simple fear of discarding today's certainties, no matter how dismal. To get them to do so, they must be presented with a convincing alternative. Even without such a campaign, several prominent Israelis have recently declared their support for one state. This is a hopeful development.

We should be under no illusion that seeking a one-state solution is a short-cut to peace. On the contrary, we need to prepare for years of sustained political struggle. But at least this path offers an alternative to violence combined with the prospect that real peace can be achieved. Persisting along the present path offers hope of neither.

Although the goal of a single, democratic and secular state was long the central platform of the Palestinian national movement, until it was abandoned in the late 1980s, Palestinian leaders made no serious effort to convince Israelis, or for that matter ordinary Palestinians, that they were not simply proposing to replace Israeli with Palestinian domination.

The burden to persuade Israelis lies largely with Palestinians, who while demanding equal rights and an end to the Jewish Israeli monopoly on power, must hold out a future in which the two communities express their identities as equals rooted by right and history in the same land.

This is undoubtedly an unfair burden, but it is a fact that oppressed groups must often show their oppressors a way out of the tunnel they have dug. This was true in South Africa, where even in the darkest days of apartheid, the African National Congress under Nelson Mandela offered white South Africans a future of reconciliation, not revenge. As in South Africa, a truth and reconciliation process can help both peoples overcome the pain of the past even as they build a just future together.

Israeli and Palestinian supporters of a one-state solution must build a new movement. This partnership must work to translate the vast international sympathy for the Palestinian cause into active support for the transformation—with international assistance and guarantees—of Israel and the Occupied Territories into a democracy for all its inhabitants. It must be a movement that builds political and moral power through non-violent resistance and civil disobedience, and mobilizes the widest possible base. Only through such a movement, I am convinced, shall we create peace in our lifetimes.

Appendix C

The One-State Solution

Virginia Tilley

There are different kinds of minorities. The notion of an Egyptian
state for the Egyptians, a Jewish state for the Jews, simply flies in the
face of reality. What we require is a rethinking of the present in terms
of coexistence and porous borders.

—Edward Said, 1999

For some years, most people sympathetic to Palestinian national aspirations—or simply alert to their durability and the political dangers they
pose—have assumed that a stable resolution of the Palestinian-Israeli conflict would require the formation of a Palestinian state in the (dwindling)
areas not yet annexed by Israel, in what is left of British Mandate territory.
This old staple of the Palestinian national movement was even belatedly
approved by Bill Clinton and then George W. Bush. The Palestinian
Authority itself was set up by the Oslo process as a pre-statal entity,
intended to establish by stages an independent Palestinian cabinet and
parliament, as a prelude to sovereignty over (a disarmed, landlocked,
dependent) Palestine. Most recently, a courageous coalition of Israeli and
Palestinian professionals has tried to imbue the two-state solution with

Source: Reprinted by permission from the *London Review of Books* 25, no.21 (2003)

new energy by formulating a detailed agreement—the so-called Geneva Accords. All these efforts have referred, vaguely or specifically, to the withdrawal of Jewish settlements, without which a Palestinian state would make no territorial sense.

Yet at some point in the past decade, this foundational precept became an obfuscating fiction. As many people privately acknowledge, and as Tony Judt has now proposed in the *New York Review of Books*, the conditions for an independent Palestinian state have been killed off by the inexorable and irreversible advance of the settlements in the West Bank and Gaza. The two-state solution to the Israeli-Palestinian conflict is an idea, and a possibility, whose time has passed, its death obscured (as was perhaps intended) by daily spectacle: the hoopla of a useless "road map," the cycles of Israeli gunship assassinations and Palestinian suicide bombings, the dismal internal Palestinian power struggles, the house demolitions and death counts—all the visible expressions of a conflict which has always been over control of land.

All the while and day by day, Israeli construction crews have been crunching and grinding through the West Bank and the Gaza Strip, laying roads and erecting thousands of new housing units in well-planned communities. "Settlement" suggests a few hilltop caravans defended by zealots, but what we have is a massive grid of towns penetrating deep into the West Bank and Gaza and now housing some 200,000 people (in addition to the 180,000 in the East Jerusalem city settlements, which no one believes will be abandoned). Tens of thousands of homes and apartments are served by schools, shopping malls, theatres and arts centres, connected by major highways, elaborate water and electricity supplies, dykes, walls, perimeter fences and surveillance systems. The grid is immovable both because of its massive infrastructure and because of the psychological investment of its residents. A decade ago, a concerted international effort might have arrested its growth. But it has now gone too far, and nothing stands in the way of its expansion.

Carved up by populous Jewish-Israeli settlements, neither the West Bank nor the Gaza Strip is a viable national territory. And it follows that if there can be no reversal of the settlement policy, a Palestinian state is not practicable. Judt believes, correctly, that the one-state solution, in whatever form (binational or ethnically cleansed), is now the only option. He has argued persuasively that Israel must confront its obsolete ethno-nationalism and face a post-Zionist vision for the country, however hard that might be. The alternative—the forced transfer of Palestinians out of the territory—is both unconscionable and unimaginably dangerous. Not surprisingly, Judt's piece has drawn fire from those who see a binational Israel as a betrayal of the promise of a Jewish haven, but as Judt points out, these objections crumble under the onslaught of 'facts on the ground'. And in any case, the ramifications of a one-state solution go far beyond Israel's existential crisis.

To consider the future of the settlements under a two-state solution is to understand that it is not a solution at all. In theory they and their 200,000 residents could be absorbed into the Palestinian state with settlers acquiring Palestinian citizenship or some kind of permanent-resident status. But given the extent of official Palestinian corruption, as well as the settlers' emotional, political and economic links to Israel, citizenship is not a serious option. Permanent residency would only compound the present situation: enclaves of non-citizens in a non-contiguous Palestinian territory. Alternatively, buildings and infrastructure could be dismantled and Jewish residents reabsorbed into Israel proper—a costly process for Israel, financially and politically. Or the settlements could simply be turned over intact for Palestinian use (helping to absorb Palestinian returnees) while Jewish residents, again, are moved into Israel proper—again, entailing major financial and political costs to Israel. The Geneva Accords are an attempt to work flexibly with these options: pulling some settlements, leaving other major ones. Yet none of the agents with the power to impose the Accords—the Israeli Government, the United States, and the European Union (or some part of it)—has the will to do so.

The present Israeli Government is not, of course, expected to undertake any such project. The problem is not merely Sharon, who has prosecuted a vigorous campaign for Israeli sovereignty over all of Mandate Palestine, of which completion of the settlement grid is a major element. Nor does the problem lie with the minority of settlers in 'Judea and Samaria' who are indeed gun-toting religious zealots (mostly from the United States), even if their domestic political influence is daunting. Should they resist removal by force, which some would certainly do, the moral authority of any government trying to shift them—even the legitimacy of the state of Israel itself—would come into question for those Zionists who understand Jewish sovereignty over the land as both right and obligation, deriving in the first instance from biblical authority and in the second from the need to safeguard Jews from contemporary anti-Semitic threats by preserving the territory as a Jewish sanctuary and homeland. Politically astute and genuinely faithful to these tenets, the religious settlers would invoke both. The uneasy compromises between Israel's secular and religious Jews could be destroyed, threatening the country's internal political fabric as well as its already faltering claim on world Jewry.

And yet the zealots are a distraction. For two decades or more, government complicity in the settlement project has far exceeded what was necessary to accommodate the extremists, and commitment to it remains embedded in government institutions and policy, beyond the reach of electoral politics. Since 1984, Sharon has served as Minister of Trade and Industry, of Construction and Housing, and of National Infrastructure. He has thus been in a position to ensure that grants and low-interest loans are available for commuter homes as well as new Israeli industry in the territories; he has expanded government involvement in providing services, banking, electricity and water supplies; facilitated private investments in housing and infrastructure; and encouraged the strategic co-operation of the Jewish Agency and World Zionist Organisation in developing settlement blocs that straddle the Green Line. Almost every government ministry and agency was involved in designing and building the Rehan bloc, for instance, which eradicated the Green Line along the north-east border of the West Bank. Reorchestrating all these agencies to cut off subsidies, services, and other incentives for settling in the territories would require altering their fundamental design (structure, policies, staff), a task beyond the ability of any Israeli politician or coalition of politicians.

To make matters worse—far worse—Israel is more zealously shielded by the United States from the political consequences of its settlement policies than it has ever been. And U.S. policy is unlikely to change. The United States will never take on the role of active peacemaker long ascribed to it by an anxious international community. Blanket support for Israel's worst actions and, recently, puerile reiterations of Sharon's insistence that Palestinians "end terror" have put paid to any hope of useful U.S. intervention; the recent attack on an American target in Gaza suggests that, even for long-credulous Palestinians, belief in Washington's role is finally collapsing. International affirmations of the importance of the United States as a broker live on because they still serve U.S. interests in pre-empting European action (and European interest in avoiding action?), while suggesting, for the especially gullible, the possibility of policy change.

None is pending, for reasons that can be found deep in the U.S. political fabric. The problem does not come down to narrow vision, or "Jewish money" (the standard anti-semitic explanation), or even to America's long-standing military strategy, which assumes Israel to be a bedrock ally— a more even-handed policy would be more likely to enhance the U.S. strategic profile than to erode it. Rather, the force durably proscribing any more constructive policy is the Congress, where one-sided support for Israel is deeply ingrained. This is the result, very largely, of Israeli-lobby leverage and campaign contributions (of various kinds) but major U.S. business interests in Israel have to be borne in mind, as does the well-organised Christian Right, with its bizarre millennialist fixation on a Jewish Israel as portending the Endtimes.

Even more limiting of U.S. foreign policy are the attitudes of individual Congressmen and women. Their public statements indicate that the great majority have internalised right-wing Israeli propaganda. For decades, the Israeli lobby has presented Congress with the narrative of a beleaguered Jewish people trying to build a homeland in a tiny country huddled on the Mediterranean while fending off irrational Islamic/Arab hostility. With members from both parties saturated in these assumptions and hooked by hard financial and electoral clout, the Presidency is greatly constrained in any attempt it might make to lever the Israeli Government towards a loathed and costly policy change—withdrawing or freezing settlements, for instance—even though there are dissenting Israelis who would ardently endorse it. Any move in this direction on the part of any President would be political suicide. The United States, then, is not neutral, but neutralised; its foreign policy remains committed to supporting Israel's "welfare" however the Israeli Government conceives it, which is why it can have no independent impact on settlement policy.

An inspirational new Palestinian leadership might have provided the moral authority to challenge the prerogatives of Israeli and U.S. strategy. It has not emerged. In restoring the authority of Arafat's corrupt inner cadre, which lacks any commitment to genuine democratic governance, the Oslo process marginalised the alternatives. Arafat himself has clung to power as crucial years have ticked by: in declining health, intoxicated by his own mystique, yet still a skilled manipulator of people and purse-strings, a decrepit godfather blocking any exit from approaching ruin. He cannot, however, contain the disintegration of the Palestinian movement from the ruins of his Ramallah offices. By physically isolating Arafat, the Sharon Government has made him powerless to control splintering Palestinian militancy and terror attacks with his old methods of pay-offs and persuasion, while leaving him in charge so that he can be blamed for them. But, confined or free, Arafat is no statesman, and has no vision appropriate to nation-building under these conditions. Yet if he were somehow to disappear quietly from the scene, as many Palestinians sincerely wish he would, his exit would leave a power vacuum which everyone rightly fears. No one in his inner circle is likely to recapture the moral high ground lost in recent years to cycles of extremist terror attacks. No alternative leader—the imprisoned Marwan Barghouti, for example—has the charisma to win the popular loyalty that might also serve to re-establish Palestinian unity. At this advanced stage of political decay, no one is in a position to step forward and take charge: those who have ventured to do so—Mahmoud Abbas, Ahmad Qurei—have rapidly withdrawn.

Israel would have little to gain from Arafat's removal. Sharon is obsessed with getting rid of him partly because he loathes him but partly, too, because he has the belief (common among Israel's right wing) that Arabs know only headman politics: a matter of self-seeking leaderships manipulating inchoate masses innately prone to 'respect power'. In this view, changing a leadership would change mass behaviour and, in the present instance, put an end to violent responses to Israeli occupation. That an Arab leadership might be politically constrained by its masses is hard for the Israeli Right to fathom, not least because it would mean accepting that the masses have developed political views and grievances of their own thanks to their first-hand experience of Israeli occupation, and of the project of the Jewish state which dispossessed them in the first place. Far from bringing about a mass change of attitude and an end to terror attacks, the removal of Arafat promises only to accelerate Palestinian political fragmentation, which may well increase, rather than diminish, terrorist attacks on Israel. In a ghastly way, however, that would suit Sharon, giving him the opportunity both to intensify the military occupation and to preserve the settlements as inviolate sanctuaries for innocent civilians threatened by barbarity.

The Palestinian national movement is in any case splintering towards anarchy. Well aware of the corruption of Arafat's cadre, and disgusted by its failure to end Israeli brutality, new extremist groups are forming every week, brandishing various ideologies of outrage, and launching wildcat actions against Israeli (and now U.S.) targets. Even Fatah is on the brink of serious splits, as successive prime ministers find themselves at the same time facing desperate demands for change and hamstrung by Arafat's controls. The Fatah-dominated elite sidelines those serious and thoughtful Palestinian intellectuals, activists and journalists who argue for alternatives. Even the best efforts of the great democratic intellectuals of the past decades—Ibrahim Abu-Lughod and Edward Said among them—could not seriously impinge on that power bloc. And those clear and principled voices have now passed, leaving in their wake equally dedicated but less authoritative figures, who—despite their best efforts—are now further enfeebled by rising Islamic militancy and the pace of political disintegration.

Sharon is nearing the realisation of his long-dreamed-of goal: Israeli sovereignty in all of Mandate Palestine, with non-viable enclaves providing a dismal Bantustan autonomy in which the remnants of Palestinian society can slowly crumble. This will leave him holding a highly undesirable package, however: a territory containing more than two million politicised Arab Muslims and Christians with no real state of their own, fragmenting Israel as effectively as Israel has fragmented their national community. The problem is as old as the conflict itself: what to do with the people, when all you want is the land?

Since forcible transfer out of the West Bank, mostly across the Jordanian border, would unleash regional violence on a scale not yet glimpsed, and since Sharon is too intelligent to pursue it, whatever the ultra-right-wing pressures on him, the Palestinians would have to remain in designated parts of the territories under some 'autonomous' Palestinian authority charged with maintaining order. Technical statehood for the Palestinians would be of no concern in this plan, as Sharon himself has stated; their economy would remain crippled, and their communities would eventually wither into irrelevant ethnic vestiges. As Judt noted, this solution might have suited the late 19th and early 20th-century ethno-nationalist ideologies that launched the Zionist movement, but it contradicts the democratic principles on which modern Israel is based. Israel's sovereignty over a West Bank containing Bantustan enclaves would entail logistical and moral impediments to its own coherence. It would also mean continued

regional unrest, with the Palestinian "plight" providing a central griev-
ance for militants throughout the Arab and Muslim world.

The real issue for the international community now is to look the one-
state solution full in the face, and sort out its obstacles. They are clearly massive. The problems for Israel are profound: compromising the Jewishness of
the "Jewish state" would not only require retooling its laws, but would run
straight up against common Zionist (and right-wing Christian) beliefs about
Israel's raison d'être. That clash is not new: it echoes the divisions in earliest
Zionist thought. The one-state solution is being mooted at a time when new
(and very emotional) debates about Israel's Jewish character have been brewing
for a decade or more, centring on "post-Zionist" queries as to whether Israel
itself can or should be reconceived: not as a Jewish state precisely (in the sense
of public institutions enshrining permanent Jewish ethno-nationalist ascen-
dancy), but as a state in which Jews are guaranteed ethnic freedoms and security on an equal basis with all citizens. It is impossible to exaggerate the extent
of the fear, sorrow, grief and outrage that run through these debates about
Israel's future or the feelings of apprehension, resentment and rejection that
talk of a secular state elicits. Yet Judt's is hardly a maverick voice, even though
Leon Wieseltier has implied as much in an irate rejoinder in the *New Republic*.

If Palestinians and Israelis (of all ethno-religious backgrounds) are
indeed to share a single state as equals, the post-Zionist vision also needs
to clarify the non-ethnic character of the Palestinian component. A formally "binational" state, recognising and reifying both Jewish and Palestinian ethno-nationalisms, could simply set up the bipolar rivalry
which, given greater Palestinian demographic weight, inspires Wieseltier
with such alarm. In his view, the domination of Jews by Palestinian
nationalism is so inevitable that it justifies the domination of Palestinians
by Jewish nationalism.

The challenge for the one-state solution is to find a political path through
the transition from rival ethno-nationalisms to a democratic secular formula
which would preserve Israel's role as a Jewish haven while dismantling the
apartheid-like privileges that presently assign second-class citizenship to
non-Jews. Israel already faces that contradiction within its legal borders:
even for the country's present Arab population, the system of laws which
safeguards the "Jewish state" are widely agreed to be unjust and in the long
run unstable. It follows that, in a democratic secular state, the very concept
of Jewish statehood (and, implicitly, the scope of Jewish nationalism) would

have to change quite radically. National rights and privileges on both sides would have to be guaranteed by subsuming them into Israeli national privileges. Benefits now legally restricted to Jews (commonly by attaching them to military service and less directly to the Law of Return), such as housing loans, education loans, public-sector employment and so forth, would have to be reconceived and resources redistributed. Land use—some 93 percent of Israel is at present reserved for Jewish use—would have to be reconfigured. Housing would have to be formally detached from exclusive Jewish occupancy (and the "Jewish-only" character of the settlements would have to evaporate). The long-established role of the Jewish Agency, which administers Jewish national resources and privileges in Israel, would have to be re-examined. Electoral politics and Knesset representation would also be transformed, to permit legislative debate on the basis of equal ethnic standing. Alterations to the Basic Laws, or the creation of a secular constitution, could ensure that Israel continues to safeguard Jewish lives and rights, providing the sanctuary which many Jews in Israel and abroad remain anxious to preserve. But the same basic law would have to ensure Muslim, Christian and, indeed, agnostic/atheist rights, and eliminate—at least juridically— any institutionalised hierarchy on ethnic or religious lines. Such a transition would require years of debate and struggle—and a political will now glaringly absent. Truth commissions and/or a general amnesty might eventually surmount the legacy of violence and hatred, but as in all such aftermaths, the process will take generations.

The problem for the Palestinians would be of a different order. Are their aspirations indeed for a democratic secular state based on territorial sovereignty—the model long proposed by Palestinian nationalists and elaborated by intellectuals such as Edward Said? Or would many now favour an ethnic or ethno-religious state based on notions of Arab and/or Muslim indigeneity of the kind taking hold in Gaza? Such a foundational debate is not unique, nor is it as hopeless as might be thought (post-apartheid South Africa has trodden some of this ground). Moreover, many Palestinians are so disillusioned with their 'national leadership' that they might welcome the idea of its demise, provided equal rights as citizens of a single state were on offer to them (finding adequate guarantees for these rights may be the primary obstacle).

The Palestinian leadership itself would probably resist such an outcome. In a one-state solution, the entire apparatus of the PLO and the PA would have to be subsumed into Israel's domestic governance and party-political processes. Many of Arafat's cronies—and his rivals—would lose major sources of economic power and political leverage in the transition. Fatah derives its economic strength from Palestinian businesses; its crony politics reflects its crucial devotion to the interests of affluent Palestinian families. Senior Fatah figures have long hoped for an independent Palestine in which, nicely positioned near the centre of power, they could flourish on the ballooning Israeli-Arab trade that peace would be expected to bring. They would sooner have a separate Palestinian state, however weak and co-opted it might be. Absorption is also a process that Israel is bound to manipulate, promoting some people and barring others from any role in the new domestic politics. Palestinians would be right to be on their guard. The Islamic militant groups, freshly inspired to see Zionism and Jews themselves as eternal enemies, would require special negotiations and treatment. The outlook may seem bleak but the prominence of the militant Islamists is quite recent and their reach much more fragile than it might seem.

The larger and longer-range impact of the one-state solution could transform regional tensions as well as local ones, by eliminating the military occupation, unifying the territory, and effectively restoring the Palestinians to (shared) sovereignty in their historical homeland. It would grant them long-sought representation, property rights, a civil justice system, and press freedoms within the democratic system hitherto reserved for Jews but which many Palestinians have long admired and hoped to emulate. It would not solve all disputes: the Haram al-Sharif/Temple Mount tensions, for example, would rumble on. But it would recast those disputes as ethnic arguments within a democratic polity rather than between polarised and mutually demonised Others. It would also return Israel to respected standing in the family of nations, and remove the "Palestinian problem" as a source of outrage for offended Muslims, Arab nationalists, and extremist groups all over the world. Given that the two-state solution promises only more trouble (and its failure will bring such dire consequences), the one-state solution is the only one that the international community can responsibly now entertain.

From the *LRB* letters page: [4 December 2003] Yitzhak Laor, Bill Templer [6 May 2004] Yisrael Medad [20 May 2004] Nicholas Blanton [3 June 2004] Virginia Tilley.

Virginia Tilley is currently working at the Centre for Policy Studies in Johannesburg. She is the author of *The One-State Solution: A Breakthrough for Peace in the Israeli-Palestinian Deadlock.*

Notes

Chapter One

1. Robert N. Rosen, *Saving the Jews: Franklin Delano Roosevelt and the Holocaust* (New York: Basic Books, 2007).
2. David Kranzler, *Holocaust Hero: Solomon Schonfeld* (Jersey City, NY: KTAV Publishing House, 2003), 46.
3. Theodore S. Hamerow, *Why We Watched: Europe, America, and the Holocaust* (New York: W. W. Norton & Company, Inc., 2008), 169–70.
4. See Jeffrey Lesser, *Welcoming the Undesirables: Brazil and the Jewish Question* (Berkeley: University of California Press, Berkeley, 1995).
5. Yad Vashem, the Holocaust Martyrs' and Heroes' Remembrance Authority, "Extract from the Speech by Adolf Hitler, January 30, 1939," http://www1.yadvashem.org.il/about_holocaust/documents/part1/doc59.html (accessed December 2008).
6. Hamerow, *Why We Watched*, xiv.
7. Statement of Mr. Francis H. Kinnicutt, "Restriction of Immigration," House Committee on Immigration and Naturalization, 68th Cong., 1st Sess. (Washington: Government Printing Office, 1924). CIS H344-2-A.
8. Patricia Clavin, "The Great Depression in Europe, 1929–39," *History Today*, no. 37 (September 2000), http://www.historytoday.com/MainArticle.aspx?m=14072&amid=14072 (accessed February 2009).

9. Fyodor Dostoyevksy, *The Diary of a Writer* (New York: Charles Scribner's Sons, 1949), 648–51.

10. See Suzanne Rutland, "Postwar Anti-Jewish Refugee Hysteria: A Case of Racial or Religious Bigotry," *Journal of Australian Studies*, no. 77 (2003).

11. The Holocaust Chronicle, "1938: The End of Illusions," http://www.holocaustchronicle.org/staticpages/122.html (accessed October 2008).

12. Professor Ben Austin, "The Forced Emigration of German Jews," Middle Tennessee State University, http://frank.mtsu.edu/~baustin/emigrate.html (accessed January 2009).

13. See Christopher R. Browning, *The Origins of the Final Solution: The Evolution of Nazi Jewish Policy, September 1939–March 1942* (Lincoln: University of Nebraska Press, 2004), 87–88.

14. Eve Nussbaum Soumerai and Carol D. Schulz, *Daily Life during the Holocaust* (Westport, CT: Greenwood Press, 1998),134.

15. Laurence Rees, *Auschwitz: A New History* (New York: Public Affairs Books, 2006), 174–75.

16. The Nizkor Project, "Joseph Goebbels' Diaries: Excerpts, 1942–43," http://www.nizkor.org/hweb/people/g/goebbels-joseph/goebbels-1948-excerpts-02.html#1942-dec-13 (accessed December 2008).

17. James Carroll, *Constantine's Sword: The Church and the Jews* (Boston: Houghton Mifflin, 2001), 522.

18. Public Broadcasting Service (PBS), "Memo from Assistant Secretary of State Breckinridge Long, to State Department Officials dated June 26, 1940, outlining effective ways to obstruct the granting of U.S. visas," http://www.pbs.org/wgbh/amex/holocaust/filmmore/reference/primary/barmemo.html (accessed September 2008)

19. PBS, "Memo to Clarence E. Pickett from Margaret E. Jones," http://www.pbs.org/wgbh/amex/holocaust/filmmore/reference/primary/barletter.html (accessed September 2008).

20. Jewish Virtual Library, "Report to the Secretary on the Acquiescence of This Government in the Murder of the Jews," http://www.jewishvirtuallibrary.org/jsource/Holocaust/treasrep.html (accessed September 2008).

21. House of Representatives, Hearings before the Committee on Immigration and Naturalization, House of Representatives, *Joint Resolution to Authorize the Admission to the United States of a Limited Number of German Refugee Children*, 244–45

22. Agostino von Hassell and Sigrid MacRae, *Alliance of Enemies* (New York: St. Martin's Press, 2006), 119.

23. Richard Breitman, *Official Secrets: What the Nazis Planned, What the British and Americans Knew* (London: Allen Penguin Press, 1998), 139.

24. "For years *Times* editors, reporters and executives tried to explain to themselves why the paper grievously underplayed the Holocaust while it was going on. Most of the world press did the same. But what mattered to us was the record of our own paper. Stories appeared now and then about Nazis killing Jews, but usually small, inside and without even trying to deal with the total horror." A. M. Rosenthal, "$5.5 Billion Missing," *New York Times*, September 24, 1996, A25.

25. Richard J. Evans, *Lying About Hitler, History, the Holocaust & the David Irving Trial* (New York: Basic Books, 2002), 129–130. David Irving was a historian who engaged in denial of the Holocaust.

26. PBS, "Memorandum: Views of the Government of the United States Regarding topics Included in the Agenda for Discussion with the British Government," http://www.pbs.org/wgbh/amex/holocaust/filmmore/reference/primary/bermmemorandum.html (accessed January 2009).

27. PBS, "Excerpt from a plan for rescue of the refugees that was submitted to the Bermuda Conference by Jewish leaders," http://www.pbs.org/wgbh/amex/holocaust/filmmore/reference/primary/bermexcerpt.html (accessed January 2009).

28. Jewish Virtual Library, "Report to the Secretary on the Acquiescence of This Government in the Murder of the Jews." http://www.jewishvirtuallibrary.org/jsource/Holocaust/treasrep.html (accessed September 2008).

29. Hamerow, *Why We Watched*.

30. David S. Wyman, "Why Auschwitz Wasn't Bombed," in *Anatomy of the Auschwitz Death Camp*, ed. Yisrael Gutman and Michael Berenbaum (Bloomington: Indiana University Press, 1998), 583.

31. Hamerow, *Why We Watched*, 309

32. Jewish Virtual Library, "Executive Order Creating the War Refugee Board," http://www.jewishvirtuallibrary.org/jsource/Holocaust/wrb1.html (accessed September 2008).

Chapter Two

1. "Foreign Secretary's Statement to the House of Commons, November 13, 1945," *Zionist Review*, November 16, 1945.

2. Jewish Virtual Library, "Report of Earl G. Harrison," http://www.jewishvirtuallibrary.orgjsourceHolocausttruman_on_harrison.html (accessed January 2009).

3. Hamerow, *Why We Watched*, 154.
4. Rutland, "Postwar Anti-Jewish Refugee Hysteria."
5. Baruch Kimmerling and Joel S. Migdal, *The Palestinian People: A History* (Cambridge, MA: Harvard University Press, 2003), 102.
6. Jewish Virtual Library, "The Peel Commission Report," http://www.jewishvirtuallibrary.org/jsource/History/peel1.html (accessed January 2009).
7. Yaakov Banai, *Chayalim Almonim* [Unknown Soldiers: The Operation Book of Lehi] (Tel Aviv: Hug Yedidem, 1987), 276.
8. Zeev Tzahor, "Holocaust Survivors as a Political Factor," *Middle Eastern Studies* 24, no. 4 (October 1988): 440.
9. Ibid.
10. Ibid., 436.
11. Jay Howard Geller, *Jews in Post-Holocaust Germany, 1945–1953* (New York: Cambridge University Press, 2005), 55
12. Ilan Pappé, "What Really Happened 50 Years Ago," *The Link* 31, no. 1 (January–March 1998), http://www.ameu.org/summary1.asp?iid=35 (accessed August 2008).
13. Peter Novick, *The Holocaust in American Life* (New York: Houghton Mifflin Company, 1999).
14. Morris L. Ernst, *So Far, So Good* (London: Falcon Press, 1953).
15. Ella Shohat, "Sephardim Israelis: Zionism from the Standpoint of Its Jewish Victims," in *Dangerous Liaisons: Gender, Nation & Postcolonial Perspectives*, ed. Ann McClintock, Aamir Mufti, and Ella Shohat (Minneapolis: University of Minnesota Press, Minneapolis, 1997), 42.
16. Ibid.
17. The one exception to the case of Zionists showing a complete disdain for the culture of their Arab neighbors was Moshe Sharett, Israel's second prime minister. He has often been painted as ineffectual and lost in the shadow of Ben-Gurion. However, Sharett had grown up in an Arab village, spoke the language fluently, had Arab friends, and according to Professor Shlaim, held a more flexible image of the Arabs than did Ben-Gurion. See Avi Shlaim, *The Iron Wall: Israel and the Arab World* (New York: W. W. Norton & Company, 2000), 96–97.
18. Ahad Ha'am, "Truth from Eretz Israel," in *Israel Studies*, ed. Gabriel Sheffer and Oren Barak (Bloomington: Indiana University Press, 2000).
19. Alan Dowty, "Much Ado about Little: Ahad Ha'am's 'Truth from Eretz Yisrael,' Zionism, and the Arabs," *Israel Studies* 5, no. 2 (2002): 156. Also see the account in Yosef Gorny, *Zionism and the Arabs, 1882–1948: A*

Study of Ideology (New York: Oxford University Press, 1987), 26–45.

20. Tzahor, "Holocaust Survivors as a Political Factor," 438.

Chapter Three

1. Avraham Burg, *The Holocaust Is Over: We Must Rise from Its Ashes* (New York: Palgrave Macmillan, 2008), 83.
2. Donald Neff, *Warriors for Jerusalem: The Six Days that Changed the Middle East* (New York: Simon & Schuster, 1984), 152.
3. Shlaim, *The Iron Wall*, 14–15.
4. Dan Kurzman, *Genesis 1948: The First Arab-Israeli War* (Ann Arbor: University of Michigan Press, 1970), 282.
5. Tom Segev, *Elvis in Jerusalem,* trans. Haim Wasman (New York: Palgrave Macmillan, 2003), 130.
6. Baruch Kimmerling, "Benny Morris's Shocking Interview," *History News Network*, January 26, 2004. http://hnn.us/articles/3166.html (accessed November 2008).
7. Benny Morris, "Revisiting the Palestinian Exodus of 1948," in *The War for Palestine: Rewriting the History of 1948*, ed. Eugene L. Rogan and Avi Shlaim (Cambridge, UK: Cambridge University Press, 2007), 38.
8. Simha Flapan, *The Birth of Israel: Myths & Realities* (New York: Pantheon, 1988), 186.
9. *Israel State Archives, Documents on the Foreign Policy of Israel (DFPI)*, Jerusalem, various dates of publication. Volumes on 1948–53, cited in Shlaim, *The Iron Wall*, p. 87.
10. Shlaim, *The Iron Wall*, 87.
11. Anton La Guardia, *War without End: Israelis, Palestinians and the Struggle for a Promised Land* (New York: St. Martin's Griffin, 2001), 164.
12. See Uri Ben-Eliezer, *The Making of Israeli Militarism* (Bloomington: Indiana University Press, 1998).
13. Thomas L. Friedman, "Rise of Militancy by Moslems Threatens Stability in Egypt," *New York Times*, October 27, 1981.
14. Bassam Tibi, *Conflict and War in the Middle East: From Interstate War to New Security* (New York: Palgrave Macmillan, 1998), 225.
15. Zachary Karabell, "Religion," in *The Columbia History of the Twentieth Century*, ed. Richard W. Bulliet (New York: Columbia University Press, 1998), 98.
16. Amnesty International, "Israel/Lebanon: Deliberate Destruction," in *The Israel Lobby and U.S. Foreign Policy*, ed. John J. Mearsheimer and Stephen M. Walt (New York: Farrar, Straus and Giroux, 2007), 320–21.

17. Mearsheimer and Walt, *The Israel Lobby*.
18. Palestine Human Rights Information Center, "Preliminary Figures through December 31, 1993," http://www.pchrgaza.org (accessed December 2008).
19. Zachary Lockman and Joel Beinin, *Intifada: The Palestinian Uprising Against Israeli Occupation* (Cambridge, MA: South End Press, 1989).
20. The Israeli Information Center for Human Rights in the Occupied Territories, http://www.btselem.org/English/index.asp (accessed November 2008).
21. Uri Avnery, "Molten Lead," *Gush-Shalom*, http://zope.gush-shalom.org/home/en/channels/avnery/1230937462/ (accessed January 2009).
22. Office of the Coordinator for Counterterrorism, "U.S. Department of State Publication 11324: Country Reports on Terrorism 2005," www.state.gov/s/ct (accessed December 2008).
23. Taghreed El-Khodary and Ethan Bronner, "Israelis Say Strikes Against Hamas Will Continue," *New York Times,* December 27, 2008, http://www.nytimes.com/2008/12/28/world/middleeast/28mideast.html?pagewanted=all (accessed January 2009).

Chapter Four
1. Daniel Schorr, "Israel's Demographic Time Bomb," *Christian Science Monitor*, August 31, 2001.
2. Richard Neuhaus, "After Israel (The Public Square: A Continuing Survey of Religion and Public Life)," *First Things: A Monthly Journal of Religion and Public Life*, April 1, 2002, http://www.articlearchives.com/society-social-assistance-lifestyle/religion-spirituality/1093637-1.html (accessed December 2008).
3. Alexander Keith, *The Land of Israel According to the Covenant with Abraham, with Isaac, and with Jacob* (New York: Harper, 1855), 43.
4. Norman Dwight Harris, *Europe and the East* (Boston: Houghton Mifflin Company, 1926), 93.
5. Ibid.
6. Steven Poole, *Unspeak: How Words Become Weapons, How Weapons Become a Message, and How that Message Becomes Reality* (New York: Grove Press, 2007), 84.
7. Jeffrey Goldberg, "Unforgiven," *The Atlantic Monthly,* May 2008.
8. Ze'ev Jabotinsky, *Medina Ivrit* [A Hebrew State], trans. Judea Pearls, in "History Disproves Myth that Founding Zionists Were Naïve," *The Jewish Journal,* May 15, 2008, http://www.jewishjournal.com/judea_pearl/page2/

history_disproves_myth_that_founding_zionists_were_naive_20080519/ (accessed November 2008).

9. Shlaim, *The Iron Wall*, 4.
10. Theodor Herzl, *Old New Land* (New York: Herzl Press, 1981).
11. Efraim Karsh, *Fabricating Israeli History: The "New Historians"* (New York: Routledge, 2000), 46–47.
12. Benny Morris, "Survival of the Fittest? An Interview with Ari Shavit," *Counterpunch,* January 16, 2004, http://www.counterpunch.org/ shavit01162004.html (accessed November 2008).
13. Goldberg, "Unforgiven."
14. Youssef Courbage, "Mirage of Palestinian Statehood: Demographic Stakes," *Le Monde Diplomatique,* April 1999.

Chapter Five

1. See Kenneth Timmerman, *Countdown to Crisis: The Coming Nuclear Showdown with Iran* (New York: Crown Forum Publishers, 2005).
2. National Intelligence Council, "Iran: Nuclear Intentions and Capabilities," *National Intelligence Estimate* (November 2007), http://www.dni.gov/press_releases/20071203_release.pdf (accessed January 2009).
3. Personal correspondence, December 2008.
4. Robert Baer, "Bet on Israel Bombing Iran," *New York Daily News*, September 27, 2008, http://www.nydailynews.com/opinions/2008/09/27/2008-09-27_bet_on_israel_bombing_iran.html (accessed October 2008). Baer cites this report: Uzi Mahnaimi and Sarah Baxter, "Revealed: Israel Plans Nuclear Strike on Iran," *London Sunday Times,* January 7, 2007, http://www.timesonline.co.uk/tol/news/world/article1290331.ece (accessed October 2008).
5. Baer, "Bet on Israel Bombing Iran."
6. Ibid.
7. Elie Leshem, "Israel Could Survive Nuclear War," *Jerusalem Post*, December 24, 2007.
8. Bronwen Maddox, "Jimmy Carter Says Israel Had 150 Nuclear Weapons," *London Times,* May 26, 2008, http://www.timesonline.co.uk/tol/news/world/middle_east/article4004300.ece (accessed October 2008).
9. Benny Morris, "The Second Holocaust Is Looming," *Israel Insider,* January 15, 2007, http://web.israelinsider.com/views/10350.htm
10. Paul Rogers, "Iran: Consequences of a War," *Briefing Paper* (Oxford: Oxford Research Group, February 2006), http:www.oxfordresearchgroup.org.uk/publications/briefing_papers/pdf/IranConsequences.pdf (accessed October 2008).

11. Philip Sherwell, "Israel Launches Covert War against Iran," *Telegraph*, February 16, 2009.

12. Ibid.

13. Goldberg, "Unforgiven."

14. Philip Roth, *Operation Shylock: A Confession* (New York: Simon & Schuster, 1993), 43.

15. Anti-Defamation League, "ADL Survey Finds Vast Majority of Israeli Teenagers Aware of Global Anti-Semitism," http://www.adl.org/PresRele/IslME_62/5014_62.htm (accessed October 2008).

16. Morris, "The Second Holocaust is Looming."

17. Grace Halsell, *Prophecy and Politics: Militant Evangelists on the Road to Nuclear War* (Westport, CT: Lawrence Hill Publishers, 1986), 121, quoted by David S. New, *Holy War: The Rise of Militant Christian, Jewish and Islamic Fundamentalism* (Jefferson, NC: McFarland & Company, Inc., Publisher, 2001), 40.

18. Donald E. Wagner, "The Evangelical-Jewish Alliance," http://www.religion-online.org/showarticle.asp?title=2717 (accessed December 2008).

19. Ibid.

20. Hal Lindsey and Carole C. Carlson, *The Late, Great Planet Earth* (Grand Rapids, MI: Zondervan, 1970).

21. Israel Shahak and Norton Mezvinsky, *Jewish Fundamentalism in Israel* (London: Pluto Press, 1999), 5–6.

22. The First or Solomon's Temple was completed in 960 BCE, according to Biblical accounts, and destroyed by the Babylonians four centuries later. The Second Temple was built in 516 BCE and destroyed by the Romans in 70 CE when they sacked Jerusalem, according to the biblical Book of Ezra.

23. Gershom Gorenberg, *The End of Days: Fundamentalism and the Struggle for the Temple Mount* (New York: Oxford University Press, 2000), 131.

24. Ibid., 136.

25. Yehuda Etzion, quoted by Ehud Sprinzak, "From Messianic Pioneering to Vigilante Terrorism: The Case of the Gush Emunim Underground," in *Inside Terrorist Organizations*, ed. David C. Rapoport (New York: Routledge, 2001), 207.

26. Gorenberg, *The End of Days*, 141.

27. See the Israeli Information Center for Human Rights in the Occupied Territories, "Statistics—Fatalities," http://www.btselem.org/English/Statistics/Casualties.asp (accessed November 2008).

28. Gorenberg, *The End of Days*, 15.

29. Serge Schmemann, "A Red Heifer, or Not? Rabbi Wonders," *New York*

Times, June 14, 1997.

30. Gorenberg, *The End of Days,* 23.

31. See Ibid.

32. Hillel Fendel, "Temple Institute Announces: High Priest's Crown Is Ready!" *Arutz Sheva/ Israel/NationalNews.com* (accessed January 2009).

33. The Temple Institute, "Sacred Vessels and Vestments," http://www.templeinstitute.org/vessels_gallery_5.htm (accessed January 2009).

34. Kobi Nahsoni, "The Sanhedrin's Peace Initiative," *Ynetnews.com* (accessed January 2009).

35. Gorenberg, *The End of Days,* 43–44.

36. David Zeidan, "A Comparative Study of Selected Themes in Christian and Islamic Fundamentalist Discourses," *British Journal of Middle Eastern Studies* 30, no. 1 (2003): 74.

37. Azzam Tamimi, "Jews and Muslims in Post-Israel Middle East," *MSANEWS,* June 30, 1999, http://msanews.mynet/Scholars/Tamimi/kitabi.html), also quoted by Ibid.

38. *Yediot Ahronot,* weekend supplement, September 18, 1998.

39. Shahak and Mezvinsky, *Jewish Fundamentalism in Israel,* 75.

40. Ibid., 76.

41. Matthew Levitt and Becca Wasser, "Violence by Extremists in the Jewish Settler Movement: A Rising Challenge," The Washington Institute, http://www.washingtoninstitute.orgtemplateC05.php?CID=2967 (accessed December 2008).

42. Karin Laub, "Olmert Decries 'Evil Wind of Extremism' in Israel," *Haaretz,* September 28, 2008.

43. Leslie Susser, "Unchecked Settler Violence Prompts Fears of Intifada," *JTA,* December 8, 2008, http://jta.org/news/article/2008/12/08/1001408/unchecked-settler-violence-prompts-fears-of-intifada (accessed December 2008).

44. Jeffrey Goldberg, "Among the Settlers: Will They Destroy Israel?" *The New Yorker,* May 31, 2004, http://www.newyorker.com/archive/2004/05/31/040531fa_fact2_a?currentPage=all (accessed December 2008).

45. Milton Viorst, "The Masada Complex," *APF Reporter* 3, no. 2 (1979), http://www.aliciapatterson.org/APF0302/Viorst/Viorst.html (accessed December 2008).

46. Ibid.

Chapter Six

1. Jeffrey Goldberg, "Unforgiven."

2. Nicholas Blanford, "Israel, Hezbollah: Has Deterrence Worked?"

Christian Science Monitor, February 13, 2009.

3. Avigail Abarbanel, "A Change Needs to Come," *Electronic Intifada,* May 26, 2008, http://www.avigailabarbanel.me.uk/charter.html (accessed December 2008).

4. Ibid.

5. H. F. Stein, "Judaism and the Group-Fantasy of Martyrdom: The Psychodynamic Paradox of Survival through Persecution," *Journal of Psychohistory* 6 (1978): 151–210.

6. Amos Elon, *The Israelis: Founders and Sons* (New York: Penguin, 1983), 198–99.

7. Daniel Bar-Tal, "Siege Mentality," in *Beyond Intractability,* ed. Guy Burgess and Heidi Burgess (Boulder: September 2004), Conflict Research Consortium, University of Colorado, http:// www.beyondintractability.org/essay/siege_mentality/?nid=1081 (accessed December 2008).

8. Doron Rosenblum, "A Right-Wing Apocalypse," *Haaretz,* October 6, 1993; also quoted by Shahak and Mezvinsky, *Jewish Fundamentalism in Israel,* 13.

9. Loren Cobb and Barbara F. Cobb, *The Persistence of War,* (Louisville, CO: Aetheling Consultants, 2005), http://www.Aetheling.com/docs/ Persistence.html (accessed September 2008).

10. David Eshel, "Terror Related Post-Traumatic Stress: The Israeli Experience," *Defense Update News Analysis,* January 6, 2007, http://www.defense-update.com/analysis/analysis_010607_ptsd.htm (accessed November 2008).

11. Ibid.

12. Ibid.

13. Yeshara Gold, "PTSD & Cockroaches," *The Jewish Magazine,* October 2002, http://www.jewishmag.com/60mag/kids4kids/kids4kids.htm (accessed November 2008).

14. Stevan E. Hobfoll, Daphna Canetti-Nisim, Robert J. Johnson, Patrick A. Palmieri, Joseph D. Varley, and Sandro Galea, "The Association of Exposure, Risk and Resiliency Factors with PTSD among Jews and Arabs Exposed to Repeated Acts of Terrorism in Israel," *Journal of Traumatic Stress* 21, no. 1 (June 2008): 9–21.

15. Evelyn Gordon, "Civil Rights: A PR Campaign that Is Three Years Too Late," *Jerusalem Post,* December 31, 2008, http://www.jpost.com/servlet/ Satellite?cid=1230733118485&pagename=JPost%2FJPArticle%2FShowFull (accessed Jauary 2009).

16. Sylvain Cypel, *Walled: Israeli Society at an Impasse* (New York: Other Press, 2005), 405.

17. Anton La Guardia, *War without End: Israelis, Palestinians, and the Struggle for a Promised Land* (New York: St. Martin's Griffin, 2001), 137.
18. See Richard Boudreaux, "Israel's Military Shame Campaign," *Los Angeles Times*, August 21, 2007.
19. "Combatants' Letter," *Courage to Refuse*, http://www.seruv.org.il/english/combatants_letter.asp (accessed December 2008).
20. Ruth Hiller and Sergeiy Sandler, "A Matter of Conscience: Militarism and Conscientious Objection to Military Service in Israel," in *Peace, Justice and Jews: Reclaiming Our Tradition*, ed. Murray Polner and Stefan Merken (New York: Bunim & Bannigan, 2007).
21. Amir Rapoport, "Suicide No. 1 Cause of Death in IDF," *Maariv International*, July 15, 2004.
22. Eyal Zisser, "Is Anyone Afraid of Israel?" *The Middle East Quarterly* 8, no. 2 (Spring 2001), http://www.meforum.org/article/24 (accessed December 2008).
23. Ibid.
24. Yoram Hazony, "The End of Zionism?" *Azure* no. 1 (Summer 1996).
25. Ibid.
26. Meyrav Wurmser, "Can Israel Survive Post-Zionism?" *Middle East Quarterly* 6, no. 1 (March 1999), http://www.meforum.org/article/469 (accessed November 2008).
27. Ibid. Also see Aharon Shabtai, "Shtei Nekudot," *Haaretz*, October 11, 1998.
28. Martin Patience, "Israel Faces Corruption 'Epidemic,'" *BBC News*, September 24, 2007, http://news.bbc.co.uk/2/hi/middle_east/6276071.stm (accessed August 2008).
29. "Olmert to Be Charged with Corruption," *London Times*, November 26, 2008, http://www.timesonline.co.uk/tol/news/world/middle_east/article5239413.ece (accessed November 2008).
30. Yanir Yagna, "Survey: 72% of Public Think Israel Is Rife with Corruption," *Haaretz*, November 11, 2005, http://www.haaretz.com/hasen/spages/1040893.html (accessed November 2008).
31. Patience, "Israel Faces Corruption 'Epidemic.'"
32. Transparency International, "2008 Corruption Perceptions Index," http://www.transparency.org/news_room/in_focus/2008/cpi2008/cpi_2008_table (accessed September 2008).
33. Haviv Rettig, "Brain Drain," *Jerusalem Post*, October 17, 2007.
34. Ibid.
35. Amir Ben-Artzi, "Israeli Brain Drain Is Cause for Concern," *EE Times*

Israel (Global News for the Creators of Technology), http://www.eetimes.eu/israel/197007599 (accessed November 2008).

36. See Jeffrey M. Peck, *Being Jewish in the New Germany* (Piscataway, NJ: Rutgers University Press, 2000).
37. Cypel, *Walled*.
38. Cited Ibid., 407.
39. David Remnick, "The Apostate: A Zionist Politician Loses Faith in the Future," *The New Yorker*, July 30, 2007.

Chapter Seven
1. Richard Cohen, "Hunker Down with History," *The Washington Post*, July 18, 2006.
2. Sidney M. Bolkosky, *The Distorted Image: German Jewish Perceptions of Germans and Germany, 1918–1935* (New York: Elsevier, 1975), 67–107.
3. Peter Loewenberg, "Review of *The Distorted Image* by Sidney M. Bolkosky," *History and Theory* 16, no. 3 (October 1977): 362.
4. Hamerow, *Why We Watched*, 186.
5. Tirza Hechter, "Historical Traumas, Ideological Conflicts, and the Process of Mythologizing," *International Journal of Middle East Studies* 35 (2003): 451.
6. Jamie Glazov, "Israel: Against All Odds," *Front Page Magazine* (January 13, 2005), http://www.frontpagemag.com/Articles/Printable.asp?ID=16627 (accessed December 2008).
7. Thomas L. Friedman, "Outsource the Cabinet?" *New York Times*, February 28, 2007.
8. Goldberg, "Unforgiven."
9. Daniel Pipes, "Israel's Substitute for Victory: Managing Conflict Without Resolving It," *Capitalism Magazine*, March 28, 2006.
10. Victor Davis Hanson, "Israel's Future," *Aish*, http://www.aish.com/jewishissues/middleeast/Israels_Future.asp (accessed September 2008).
11. Yossi Melman, "Syria Reportedly Stepping up Production of Chemical Weapons," *Haaretz*, February 18, 2009.
12. Uzi Mahnaimi and Sarah Baxter, "Israelis Seized Nuclear Material in Syrian Raid," *Times Online*, September 23, 2007, http://www.timesonline.co.uk/tol/news/world/middle_east/article2512380.ece (accessed November 2008).
13. Barry Rubin, "Israel's Grand Strategy," *Israel Insider*, August 18, 2008, http://web.israelinsider.com/Views/13063.htm (accessed November 2008).

14. See John J. Mearsheimer and Stephen M. Walt, *The Israel Lobby and U.S. Foreign Policy* (New York: Farrar, Straus and Giroux, 2007).

15. Will Kymlicka, *Liberalism, Community and Culture* (Oxford: Clarendon Press, 1989), 146.

16. Daniel Gordis, "When Magical Thinking Will Not Suffice: Israeli Democracy, Israeli Arabs and the Kinneret Agreement," in *Renewing the Jewish Social Contract: Bridging the Religious Secular Divide*, American Jewish Committee, http://www.ajc.org/site/apps/nlnet/content3.aspx?c=ijITI2PHKoG&b=843137&ct=6313193 (accessed December 2008).

17. Daniel Pipes, "Does Israel Need a Plan?" http://www.danielpipes.org/article/1015

18. Akiko Fukushima, "Understanding and Addressing the Underlying Causes of International Terrorism," http://www.yorku.ca/yciss/activities/documents/CanadaJapanUnderstandingandAddressing.pdf (accessed December 2008).

19. John Mearsheimer and Stephen Walt, "The Israel Lobby," *London Review of Books*, March 23, 2006, http://www.lrb.co.uk/v28/n06/mear01_.html (accessed December 2008).

20. Immanuel Wallerstein, "Last Call for a Two-state Solution," *International Herald Tribune*, November 1, 2007.

21. Jeff Halper, "The 94 Percent Solution: A Matrix of Control," *Middle East Report,* no. 216 (Fall 2000).

22. Halper, "The 94 Percent Solution."

23. Daniel Seidemann, "Letting Israel Self-Destruct," *The Washington Post*, August 26, 2004, http://www.washingtonpost.com/ac2/wp-dyn/A34025-2004Aug25?language=printer (accessed November 2008).

24. Saree Makdisi, "Forget the Two-State Solution," *Los Angeles Times*, May 11, 2008, and United Nations Office for the Coordination of Humanitarian Affairs "The Humanitarian Impact on Palestinians of Israeli Settlements and Other Infrastructure in the West Bank," http://www.ochaopt.orgdocumentsTheHumanitarianImpactOfIsraeliInfrastructure TheWestBank_full.pdf (accessed September 2008).

25. Jimmy Carter, *Palestine: Peace Not Apartheid* (New York: Simon & Schuster, 2006), 215.

26. See Benjamin Pogrund, "Israel Is a Democracy in Which Arabs Vote—Not an Apartheid State," *Focus 40,* December 2005, http://www.zionism-israel.com/ezine/Israel_democracy.htm (accessed December 2008).

27. Leila Farsakh, "Under Siege: Closure, Separation and the Palestinian

Economy," *Middle East Report*, no. 217 (Winter 2000), http://www.merip.org/mer/mer217/217_farsakh.html (accessed October 2008).

28. See Peter Liberman, "The Rise and Fall of the South African Bomb," *International Security* 26, no. 2 (Fall 2001), 45–86.

29. Laila El-Haddad, "The One-State Solution," *Aljazeera*, http://english.aljazeera.net/news/middleeast/2007/06/2008525173524816580.html (accessed September 2008).

30. Yoram Hazony, *The Jewish State: The Struggle for Israel's Soul* (New York: Basic Books, 2000), xxvi.

31. Ibid., xxvi.

32. See Ernest Renan, "What Is a Nation?" in *Nation and Narration*, ed. Homi Bhabha (London: Routledge, 1990), 19–20.

Chapter Eight

1. Burg, *The Holocaust Is Over*, 80.
2. Uri Ram, "The Future of the Past in Israel—A Sociology of Knowledge Approach," in *Making Israel*, ed. Benny Morris (Ann Arbor: University of Michigan Press, 2007), 210–11.
3. Gorenberg, *The End of Days*, 114
4. Ofira Seliktar, "The New Zionism," *Foreign Policy*, no. 51 (Summer 1983): 132.
5. See Mearsheimer and Walt, *The Israel Lobby and U.S. Foreign Policy*.
6. Juan Cole, "Neoconservatism Dies in Gaza," *Salon*, January 8, 2009, http://www.salon.com/opinion/feature/2009/01/08/gaza/index.html (accessed January 2009).
7. Dan Froomkin, "Let's Hear from Someone Besides the Neoconservatives about Iran," *Nieman Watchdog*, August 20, 2007, http://niemanwatchdog.orgindex.cfm?fuseaction=background.view&backgroundid=00203 (accessed October 2008).
8. Alec Magnet, "Support of Israel Declining among Young Jewish Americans, Poll Says," *New York Sun*, December 2, 2005.
9. Michael Conlon, "Study Finds U.S. Jews Distance Selves from Israel," *Reuters*, September 6, 2007, http://www.reuters.com/article/domesticNews/idUSN0439419520070906 (accessed January 2009).
10. Jeet Heer, "Losing the PR War and the Diaspora," *National Post, Canada*, January 9, 2009, http://www.nationalpost.com/story.html?id=1158883 (accessed January 2009).
11. Shahak and Mezvinsky, *Jewish Fundamentalism in Israel*, 18
12. See "Neturei Karta International—Jews United Against Zionism," http://www.nkusa.org/ (accessed December 2008).
13. Yakov M. Rabkin, *A Threat from Within: A Century of Jewish Opposi-*

tion to Zionism (London: Zed Books, 2006).

14. Rabbi Lisa Hochberg-Miller, "High Holiday Sermons," http://www.cipcug.org/minkin/TBT/RABLHM/hhdsermons.html.

15. Morris, *Making Israel*, 14–15.

16. See Yehouda Shenhav, "The Bond of Silence," *Haaretz*, December 26, 1996.

17. Deborah L. Wheeler, "Does Post-Zionism Have a Future?" in *Traditions and Transitions in Israel Studies*, ed. Laura Z. Eisenberg, Neil Caplan, Naomi B. Sokoloff, and Mohammed Abu-Nimer (New York: SUNY Press, 2003), 166.

18. Avraham Burg, "The End of Zionism: Israel Must Shed Its Illusions and Choose between Racist Oppression and Democracy," *The (London) Guardian*, September 15, 2003.

19. Remnick, "The Apostate."

20. Peter Hirchberg, "One-State Awakening," *Haaretz*, October 12, 2003, http://www.haaretz.com/hasen/pages/ShArt.jhtml?itemNo=370673 (accessed January 2009).

21. Edward Said, "Bases of Coexistence," *Al-Hayat*, November 1997, and Ali Abunimah, *One Country: A Bold Proposal to End the Israeli-Palestinian Impasse* (New York: Metropolitan Books, 2006), 169.

22. Tony Judt, "Israel: The Alternative," *The New York Review of Books*, October 23, 2003.

23. Ibid.

24. Martin Sherman, "Post-Zionism's Fatal Flaw," http://www.ynetnews.com/articles/0,7340,L-3580743,00.html (accessed August 21, 2008).

Chapter Nine

1. Dalia Shehori, "Post-Zionism Is Dead or in a Deep Freeze," *Haaretz*, April 20, 2004.

2. Ami Isseroff, "Post-Zionism: Requiem for an Intellectual Fad," http://www.mideastweb.org/log/archives/00000247.htm (Accessed November 2008).

3. Ari Shavit, "Survival of the Fittest? An Interview with Benny Morris," *Haaretz*, January 6, 2004.

4. Aluf Benn, David Landau, Barak Ravid, and Shmuel Rosner, "Olmert to Haaretz: Two-State Solution or Israel is Done For," *Haaretz*, November 29, 2007.

5. Institute for Middle East Understanding, "The Declaration," http://imeu.net/news/article007179.shtml (accessed November 2008).

6. John Strawson, review of *The One-State Solution: A Breakthrough Plan*

for Peace in the Israeli-Palestinian Deadlock by Virginia Tilley, *Democratiya* (Spring 2006), http://www.democratiya.com/review.asp?reviews_id=23 (accessed November 2008).

7. Gary Selikow, "Recipe for a Second Holocaust," Review of *The One State Solution* by Virginia Tilley, posted June 2, 2008, http://www.amazon.co.uk/One-State-Solution-Virginia-Q-Tilley/dp/0472115138 (accessed November 2008).

8. Abunimah, *One Country: A Bold Proposal to End the Israeli-Palestinian Impasse.*

9. Isabel Kershner, "Noted Arab citizens call on Israel to shed Jewish identity," *International Herald Tribune*, February 8, 2007.

10. Ghada Karmi, *Married to Another Man: Israel's Dilemma in Palestine* (London: Pluto Press, 2007).

11. Ibid.

12. Private email correspondence, October 14, 2008.

13. "Or Commission Report," *Israel Studies* 11, no. 2 (July 2006): 25–53

14. Adalah, *Legal Violations of Arab Minorities in Israel: A Report on Israel's Implementation of the International Convention on the Elimination of all Forms of Racial Discrimination*, http://www.adalah.org/eng/publications/violations.htm (accessed October 2008).

15. "A One-State Solution: Advocating Israel's Destruction," *Honest Reporting*, October 24, 2007, http://www.honestreporting.com/articles/45884734/critiques/new/A_OneState_Solution_Advocating_Israels_Destruction_.asp (accessed September 2008).

16. Sol Stern and Fred Siegal, "Mideast Parley Takes Ugly Turn at Columbia University," *New York Sun*, February 4, 2005.

17. Mark Satin, "The One State Solution Is the Most Visionary and the Most Sensible," *Radical Middle Newsletter*, April 2007, http://www.radicalmiddle.com/x_onestate.htm (accessed October 2008).

18. George E. Bisharat, "A Two-State or One-State Solution?" *Los Angeles Times*, May 14, 2008, http://www.latimes.com/news/opinion/la-op-pearl-bisharat14-2008may14,0,2612452,full.story (accessed November 2008).

19. Muammar Qaddafi, "The One-State Solution," *New York Times,* January 21, 2009.

20. Uri Avnery, "Uri Avnery on the One State Solution," *Israel News*, May 12, 2007, http://zionism-israel.com/israel_news/2007/05/uri-avnery-on-one-state-solution.html (accessed September 2008)

21. Hillel Halkin, "If Israel Ceased to Exist," in *The Jewish Condition: Challenges & Responses, 1938–2008*, ed. William Helmreich, Mark

Rosenblum, and David Schimel (Piscataway, NJ: Transaction Publishers, 2008), 128.

22. Richard Boudreaux and Ashraf Khalil, "For Some Palestinians, One State with Israel Is Better than None," *Los Angeles Times,* May 8, 2008.

23. Ibid.

24. Abunimah, *One Country,* 164.

25. Virginia Tilley, "The Secular Solution," *The New Left Review,* no. 38 (March–April 2006), http://www.newleftreview.org/A2607 (accessed November 2008).

26. Benjamin Pogrund, "Israel Is a Democracy in which Arabs Vote.

27. Ilan Pappé, "Looking for Alternatives to Failure: An Answer to Uri Avnery."

28. Ali Abunimah, "Palestine/Israel: One State for All Its Citizens," *The Electronic Intifada,* October 16, 2003, http://odspi.org/articles/abunimah.html (accessed December 2008).

29. Uri Avnery, "The Bed of Sodom," *Gush Shalom,* http://zope.gush-shalom.org/home/en/channels/avnery/1177227796/ (accessed December 2008).

30. Abunimah, *One Country,* 171.

31. Pappé, "Looking for Alternatives to Failure," *Electronic Intifada,* April 26, 2007, http://electronicintifada.net/v2/article6836.shtml (accessed December 2008).

32. For more details of this strategy, see Satin, "The One State Solution Is the Most Visionary and the Most Sensible."

Chapter Ten

1. See Wyndham Lewis, *The Jews, Are They Human?* (London: George Allen & Unwin, 1939).

2. Burg, *The Holocaust Is Over,* 78.

3. Ibid., 100.

4. Ilan Pappé, "As Long as the Plan Contains the Magic Term 'Withdrawal,' It Is Seen as a Good Thing," *London Review of Books,* May 6, 2004.

5. Mearsheimer and Walt, *The Israel Lobby.*

6. Segev, *Elvis in Jerusalem,* 75.

7. Daniel Seidemann, "Letting Israel Self-Destruct," *The Washington Post,* August 6, 2004.

8. Jay Bookman, "Israel Cannot 'Free' Gaza of Hamas with War," *Atlanta*

Journal-Constitution, January 8, 2009.

9. Eliat Gordin Levitan, "Ginsburg Family," http://www.eilatgordinlevitan.com/kurenets/k_pages/ginsburg.html (accessed January 2009).

10. Burg, *The Holocaust is Over,* 144.

11. See Thomas Cahill, *The Gifts of the Jews: How a Tribe of Desert Nomads Changed the Way Everyone Thinks and Feels,* (New York: Anchor Books, 1999).

12. Burg, *The Holocaust Is Over.*

13. Meron Benvenisti, "Which Kind of Binational State?" *Haaretz,* November 20, 2003.

14. Mahdi Abdul Hadi, ed., *Palestinian-Israeli Impasse: Exploring Alternative Solutions to the Palestine-Israel Conflict* (Jerusalem: PASSIA Publications, 2005).

15. Gary Sussman, "The Challenge to the Two-State Solution," *Middle East Report,* no. 231 (Summer 2004), http://www.merip.org/mer/mer231/sussman.html (accessed November 2008).

16. Jeff Halper, "End of the Road Map: Preparing for the Struggle against Apartheid," *Counterpunch,* September 19, 2003, http://www.counterpunch.org/halper09192003.html (accessed November 2008).

17. Abunimah, *One Country,* 115.

18. Yakov M. Rabkin, "A Glimmer of Hope, A State of All Its Citizens," *Tikkun: A Bimonthly Jewish Critique of Politics, Culture & Society* (July–August 2002), http://odspi.org/articles/rabkin.html (accessed November 2008).

19. Ibid.

20. Mark LeVine, "The State of Israel-Palestine," *History News Network,* July 20, 2006, http://hnn.us/blogs/entries/28707.html (accessed November 2008).

21. See Howard Cort, "Alternative Approaches to Palestinian-Israeli Coexistence," http://www.middleeast.orglaunchredirect.cgi?num=582&a=66 (accessed November 2008).

22. Meron Benvenisti, "Cry the Beloved Two-State Solution," *Haaretz,* August 6, 2003.

23. Cort, "Alternative Approaches to Palestinian-Israeli Coexistence."

Appendix A

1. "The One State Declaration," *The Electronic Intifada*, November 29, 2007, http://electronicintifada.net/v2/article9134.shtml (accessed September 2008).

Appendix B

1. Abunimah, "Palestine/Israel: One State for All its Citizens."

Selected Bibliography

Abdul, Hadi Madhi. *Palestinian-Israeli Impasse: Exploring Alternative so-lutions to the Palestine-Israel Conflict.* Jerusalem: PASSIA Publications, 2005.

———. "The One-State Solution." Interview by Laila El-Haddad. *Al Jazeera.* June 29, 2009. http://english.aljazeera.net/news/middleeast/ 2007/06/2008525173524816580.html

———. *One Country: A Bold Proposal to End the Israeli-Palestinian Impasse.* New York: Metropolitan Books, 2006.

Adalah. *Legal Violations of Arab Minorities in Israel: A Report on Israel's Imple-mentation of the International Convention on the Elimination of All Forms of Racial Discrimination.* Israel: Adalah, 1998.

Amnesty International. *Lebanon: Deliberate Destruction or "Collateral Dam-age"? Israeli Attacks on Civilian Infrastructure.* Amnesty International, MDE Report 18/007/2006, 2006.

Banai, Yaakov. *Chayalim Almonim* [Unknown Soldiers: The Operation Book of Lehi]. Tel Aviv: Hug Yedidem, 1987.

Ben-Eliezer, Uri. *The Making of Israeli Militarism.* Bloomington: Indiana University Press, 1998.

Blanford, Nicholas. "Israel, Hezbollah: Has Deterrence Worked?" *Christian Science Monitor,* February 13, 2009.

Bolkosky, Sidney M. *The Distorted Image: German Jewish Perceptions of Germans and Germany, 1918–1935.* New York: Elsevier, 1975.

Browning, Christopher R. *The Origins of the Final Solution: The Evolution of Nazi Jewish Policy, September 1939–March 1942.* Lincoln: University of Nebraska Press, 2004.

Burg, Avraham. "The Apostate: A Zionist Politician Loses Faith in the Future." Interview by David Remnick. *The New Yorker.* July 30, 2007.

———. *The Holocaust Is Over: We Must Rise from Its Ashes.* New York: Palgrave Macmillan, 2008.

Carroll, James. *Constantine's Sword: The Church and the Jews.* Boston: Houghton Mifflin, 2001.

Carter, Jimmy. *Palestine: Peace Not Apartheid.* New York: Simon & Schuster, 2006.

Cobb, Loren, and Barbara F. Cobb. *The Persistence of War.* Lousiville, CO: Aetheling Consultants, 2005.

"Combatants' Letter," *Courage to Refuse.* http://www.seruv.org.il/english/ combatants_letter.asp (accessed December 2008).

"Combatants' Letter,"

Dostoyevksy, Fyodor. *The Diary of a Writer.* New York: Charles Scribner's Sons, 1949.

Dowty, Alan. "Much Ado about Little: Ahad Ha'am's 'Truth from Eretz Yisrael,' Zionism, and the Arabs." *Israel Studies* 5, no. 2 (2000).

Elon, Amos. *The Israelis: Founders and Sons.* New York: Penguin, 1983.

Ernst, Morris L. *So Far, So Good.* London: Falcon Press, 1953.

Etzion, Yehuda, quoted by Ehud Sprinzak. "From Messianic Pioneering to Vigilante Terrorism: The Case of the Gush Emunim Underground." In *Inside Terrorist Organizations*, edited by David C. Rapoport. New York: Routledge, 2001.

Farsakh, Leila. "Under Siege: Closure, Separation and the Palestinian Economy." *Middle East Report*, no. 217 (Winter 2000).

Flapan, Simha. *The Birth of Israel: Myths & Realities.* New York: Pantheon, 1988.

Geller, Jay Howard. *Jews in Post-Holocaust Germany, 1945–1953.* New York: Cambridge University Press, 2005.

Goldberg, Jeffrey. "Unforgiven." *The Atlantic Monthly*, May 2008, http:// www.theatlantic.com/doc/print/200805/israel (October 2008).

Gorenberg, Gershom. *The End of Days: Fundamentalism and the Struggle for the Temple Mount.* New York: Oxford University Press, 2000.

Gorny, Yosef. *Zionism and the Arabs, 1882–1948: A Study of Ideology.* New York: Oxford University Press, 1987.

Ha'am, Ahad. "Truth from Eretz Israel." In *Israel Studies*, ed. Gabriel Sheffer and Oren Barak. Bloomington: Indiana University Press, 2000.

Halkin, Hillel. "If Israel Ceased to Exist." In *The Jewish Condition: Challenges & Responses, 1938–2008*, edited by William Helmreich, Mark Rosenblum, and David Schimel. Piscataway, NJ: Transaction Publishers, 2008.

Halper, Jeff. "The 94 Percent Solution: A Matrix of Control." *Middle East Report,* no. 216 (Fall 2000).

Halsell, Grace. *Prophecy and Politics: Militant Evangelists on the Road to Nuclear War.* Westport, CT: Lawrence Hill Publishers, 1986.

Hamerow, Theodore S. *Why We Watched: Europe, America, and the Holocaust.* New York: W. W. Norton & Company, Inc., 2008.

Harris, Norman Dwight. *Europe and the East.* Boston: Houghton Mifflin Company, 1926).

Hazony, Yoram. "The End of Zionism?" *Azure*, no. 1 (Summer 1996).

————. *The Jewish State: The Struggle for Israel's Soul.* New York: Basic Books, 2000.

Hechter, Tirza. "Historical Traumas, Ideological Conflicts, and the Process of Mythologizing," *International Journal of Middle East Studies* 35 (2003).

Herzl, Theodor. *Old New Land.* New York: Herzl Press, 1981.

Hiller, Ruth, and Sergeiy Sandler. "A Matter of Conscience: Militarism and Conscientious Objection to Military Service in Israel." In *Peace, Justice and Jews: Reclaiming Our Tradition*, edited by Murray Polner and Stefan Merken. New York: Bunim & Bannigan, 2007.

Hobfoll, Stevan E., Daphna Canetti-Nisim, Robert J. Johnson, Patrick A. Palmieri, Joseph D. Varley, and Sandro Galea. "The Association of Exposure, Risk and Resiliency Factors with PTSD among Jews and Arabs Exposed to Repeated Acts of Terrorism in Israel." *Journal of Traumatic Stress* 21, no. 1 (June 2008).

Israel State Archives. *Documents on the Foreign Policy of Israel (DFPI).* Jerusalem: various dates of publication.

Jabotinsky, Ze'ev. *Medina Ivrit* [A Hebrew State]. Translated by Judea Pearl. In "History Disproves Myth that Founding Zionists Were Naïve." *The Jewish Journal,* May 15, 2008, http://www.jewishjournal.com/judea_pearl/page2history_disproves_myth_that_founding_zionists_were_naive_20080519/ (accessed November 2008).

Judt, Tony. "Israel: The Alternative." *The New York Review of Books*, October 23, 2003.

Karmi, Ghada. *Married to Another Man: Israel's Dilemma in Palestine.* London: Pluto Press, 2007.

Karsh, Efraim. *Fabricating Israeli History: The "New Historians."* New York: Routledge, 2000.

Keith, Alexander. *The Land of Israel According to the Covenant with Abraham, with Isaac, and with Jacob.* New York: Harper, 1855.

Kimmerling, Baruch. "Benny Morris's Shocking Interview." *History News Network*, January 26, 2004. http://hnn.us/articles/3166.html (accessed November 2008).

Kimmerling, Baruch, and Joel S. Migdal. *The Palestinian People: A History.* Cambridge, MA: Harvard University Press, 2003.

Kranzler, David. *Holocaust Hero: Solomon Schonfeld.* Jersey City, NJ: KTAV Publishing House, 2003.

Kurzman, Dan. *Genesis 1948: The First Arab-Israeli War.* Ann Arbor: University of Michigan Press, 1970.

Kymlicka, Will. *Liberalism, Community and Culture.* New York: Clarendon Press, 1989.

La Guardia, Anton. *War without End: Israelis, Palestinians and the Struggle for a Promised Land.* New York: St. Martin's Griffin, 2001.

LeVine, Mark. "The State of Israel-Palestine." *History News Network*, July 20, 2006.

Lewis, Wyndham. *The Jews, Are They Human?* London: George Allen & Unwin, 1939.

Lindsey, Hal, and Carole C. Carlson. *The Late, Great Planet Earth.* Grand Rapids, MI: Zondervan, 1970.

Lockman, Zachary, and Joel Beinin. *Intifada: The Palestinian Uprising against Israeli Occupation.* Cambridge, MA: South End Press, 1989.

Loewenberg, Peter. "Review of *The Distorted Image* by Sidney M. Bolkosky." In *History and Theory* 16, no. 3 (October 1977).

Long, Breckinridge. "Memo from Assistant Secretary of State Breckinridge Long, to State Department Officials dated June 26, 1940, outlining effective ways to obstruct the granting of U.S. visas." http://www.pbs.org/wgbh/amex/holocaust/filmmore/reference/primary/barmemo.html (accessed September 2008).

McClintock, Ann, Aamir Mufti, Ella Shohat, Eds. *Dangerous Liaisons: Gender, Nation & Postcolonial Perspectives.* Minneapolis: University of Minnesota Press, 1997.

Mearsheimer, John J. and Stephen M Walt. *The Israel Lobby and U.S. Foreign Policy.* New York: Farrar, Straus and Giroux, 2007.

Morris, Benny. *Making Israel.* Ann Arbor: University of Michigan Press, 2007.

———. "Revisiting the Palestinian Exodus of 1948." In *The War for*

Palestine: Rewriting the History of 1948, edited by Eugene L. Rogan and Avi Shlaim. Cambridge, UK: Cambridge University Press, 2007.

Neff, Donald. *Warriors for Jerusalem: The Six Days that Changed the Middle East.* New York: Simon & Schuster, 1984.

Neturei Karta International—Jews United Against Zionism. http://www.nkusa.org/

Neuhaus, Richard. "After Israel (The Public Square: A Continuing Survey of Religion and Public Life)." *First Things: A Monthly Journal of Religion and Public Life,* April 1, 2002, http://www.articlearchives.com/society-social-assistance-lifestyle/religion-spirituality/1093637-1.html (accessed December 2008).

New, David S. *Holy War: The Rise of Militant Christian, Jewish and Islamic Fundamentalism.* Jefferson, NC: McFarland & Company, Inc., Publisher, 2001).

Novick, Peter. *The Holocaust in American Life.* New York: Houghton Mifflin Company, 1999.

Pappé, Ilan. "What Really Happened 50 Years Ago." *The Link* 31, no. 1 (January–March 1998), http://www.ameu.org/summary1.asp?iid=35 (accessed August 2008).

Patience, Martin, "Israel Faces Corruption Epidemic." *BBC News,* September 24, 2007. http://news.bbc.co.uk/2/hi/middle_east/6276071.stm (accessed August 2008).

Peck, Jeffrey M. *Being Jewish in the New Germany.* Piscataway, NJ: Rutgers University Press, 2000.

Pogrund, Benjamin. "Israel Is a Democracy in Which Arabs Vote—Not an Apartheid State." *Focus 40,* December 2005, http://www.zionism-israel.com/ezine/Israel_democracy.htm (accessed December 2008).

Poole, Stephen. *Unspeak: How Words Become Weapons, How Weapons Become a Message, and How that Message Becomes Reality.* New York: Grove Press, 2007.

Rabkin, Yakov M. *A Threat From Within: A Century of Jewish Opposition to Zionism.* London: Zed Books, 2006.

Ram, Uri. "The Future of the Past in Israel—A Sociology of Knowledge Approach." In *Making Israel,* edited by Benny Morris. Ann Arbor: University of Michigan Press, 2007. Rees, Laurence. *Auschwitz: A New History.* New York: PublicAffairs Books, 2006.

Renan, Ernest. "What Is a Nation?" In *Nation and Narration,* edited by Homi Bhabha. London: Routledge, 1990.

Roth, Philip. *Operation Shylock: A Confession.* New York: Simon & Schuster, 1993.

Rutland, Suzanne. "Postwar Anti-Jewish Refugee Hysteria: A Case of Racial or Religious Bigotry." *Journal of Australian Studies*, no. 77 (2003).

Schorr, Daniel. "Israel's Demographic Time Bomb." *Christian Science Monitor*. August 31, 2001.

Segev, Tom. *Elvis in Jerusalem: Post-Zionism and the Americanization of Israel*. Translated by Haim Watzerman. New York: Holt Paperbacks, 2002.

Selikow, Gary. "Recipe for a Second Holocaust." Review of *The One State Solution*, by Virginia Tilley, June 2, 2008, http://www.amazon.co.uk/One-State-Solution-Virginia-Q-Tilley/dp/0472115138 (accessed November 2008).

Seliktar, Ofira. "The New Zionism." *Foreign Policy*, no. 51 (Summer 1983).

Shahak, Israel and Norton Mezvinsky. *Jewish Fundamentalism in Israel*. London: Pluto Press, 1999.

Shlaim, Avi. *The Iron Wall: Israel and the Arab World*. New York: W. W. Norton & Company, 2000.

Shohat, Ella. "Sephardim Israelis: Zionism from the Standpoint of Its Jewish Victims." In *Dangerous Liaisons: Gender, Nation, and Postcolonial Perspectives*, edited by Anne McClintock, Aamir Mufti, and Ella Shohat. Minneapolis: University of Minnesota Press, 1997.

Soumerai, Eve Nussbaum, and Carol D. Schulz. *Daily Life during the Holocaust*. Westport, CT: Greenwood Press, 1998.

Stein, H.F. "Judaism and the Group-Fantasy of Martyrdom: The Psychodynamic Paradox of Survival Through Persecution." *Journal of Psychohistory* 6 (1978).

Strawson, John. Book review of *The One State Solution*, by Virginia Tilley, Spring 2006, http://www.democratiya.com/review.asp?reviews_id=23 (accessed November 2008).

Tibi, Bassam. *Conflict and War in the Middle East: From Interstate War to New Security*. New York: Palgrave Macmillan, 1998).

Tilley, Virginia. "The Secular Solution." *The New Left Review*, no. 38 (March–April 2006), http://www.newleftreview.org/A2607 (accessed November 2008).

Timmerman, Kenneth. *Countdown to Crisis: The Coming Nuclear Showdown with Iran*. New York: Crown Forum Publishers, 2005.

Tzahor, Zeev. "Holocaust Survivors as a Political Factor." *Middle Eastern Studies* 24, no. 4 (October 1988).

Von Hassell, Agostino and Sigrid MacRae. *Alliance of Enemies*. New York: St. Martin's Press, 2006.

Wheeler, Deborah L. "Does Post-Zionism Have a Future?" In *Traditions and*

*Transitions in Israel Studies*m, edited by Laura Z. Eisenberg, Neil Caplan, Naomi B. Sokoloff, Mohammed Abu-Nimer. New York: SUNY Press, 2003.

Wurmser, Meyrav. "Can Israel Survive Post-Zionism?" *The Middle East Quarterly* 6, no. 1 (March 1999), http://www.meforum.org/article/469 (accessed November 2008).

Yad Vashem. The Holocaust Martyrs' and Heroes' Remembrance Authority. "Extract from the Speech by Adolf Hitler, January 30, 1939." Http://www1.yadvashem.org.il/about_holocaust/documents/part1/doc59.html (accessed December 2008).

Zisser, Eyal. "Is Anyone Afraid of Israel?" *The Middle East Quarterly*, Spring 2001, http://www.meforum.org/article/24 (accessed December 2008).

Index

About the Author

Constance Hilliard is a professor of African and Middle Eastern history at the University of North Texas, Denton. She holds a doctorate in Middle East and African history from Harvard University and is a former foreign policy adviser to the late Senator John Tower, who chaired the Senate Armed Services Committee. She lives in Hickory Creek, Texas.